Emotional Development, Theory and Applications

Emotional Development, Theory and Applications

A Neo-Piagetian Perspective

Henry Dupont

 PRAEGER

Westport, Connecticut
London

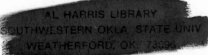

Library of Congress Cataloging-in-Publication Data

Dupont, Henry.
    Emotional development, theory and applications : a neo-
Piagetian perspective / Henry Dupont.
      p.   cm.
    Includes bibliographical references and index.
    ISBN 0–275–94839–0 (alk. paper)
    1. Emotions in children. 2. Piaget, Jean, 1896– . I. Title.
BF723.E6D87   1994
155.4′124—dc20   93–43067

British Library Cataloguing in Publication Data is available.

Library of Congress Catalog Card Number: 93–43067
ISBN: 0–275–94839–0

First published in 1994

Praeger Publishers, 88 Post Road West, Westport, CT 06881
An imprint of Greenwood Publishing Group, Inc.

Printed in the United States of America

The paper used in this book complies with the
Permanent Paper Standard issued by the National
Information Standards Organization (Z39.48–1984).

10 9 8 7 6 5 4 3 2 1

This book is dedicated to the following people in acknowledgment of their contribution to my professional development and to my efforts to produce this book:

Nicholas Hobbs
Theodore Landsman
Julius Seeman
William Rhodes
Ralph Mosher
Norman Sprinthall
Bruce Pemberton
R. Dale Dick
John LeCapitaine
Lamar Gordon

and, in a very special way, to Christine Dupont without whose assistance the book would never have been written.

Contents

Contents

Tables

Preface

My very first professional experience involved doing play therapy with children while teaching human development as a member of the College of Education faculty at the University of Delaware. This first experience left me interested in human emotions and their development. I was puzzled by the fact that there was no theory of emotional development as such, and that emotion was regarded as too soft a topic for serious study.

When I studied psychoanalytic theory I discovered that, according to Freud, our emotions do not change; they are instinctive and innate, and they are just transferred from one object to another in the course of our development so no theory about their development was needed.

The work of Tomkins (1962, 1963) proved interesting for its emphasis on primary affects, but his work focused essentially on the delineation of the primary emotions (affects) in studies of facial expressions across cultures, and not on their development.

Izard's (1977) differential emotions theory, building to some degree on the work of Tomkins (1962, 1963), was more of a topography of human emotions than a theory about their development. This work and his more recent work (Izard & Malatesta, 1987) are limited by an emphasis on the developmental course of facial expressions and what appears to be a reification of emotion, that is, the practice of regarding emotions as real entities rather than as functional processes.

Cognitive theories of emotion have focused on the relationship between cognition and emotion (Arnold, 1960) and on cognition, emotion, and the person-environment relationship described by Lazarus (1991a, 1991b), but neither this work nor that of Ellis (1962, 1985) has produced a theory of emotional development.

Lewis and Michalson (1983) presented a structural model of emotion and then described "the emergence and the unfolding of a particular emotion in both children and adults" (p. 129). Their emphasis, however, was on the socialization of emotion, particularly its expression, and as interesting and informative as that was, it did not represent a theory of emotional development. They suggested that "a comprehensive theory . . . may never be available" (Lewis & Michalson, 1983, p. 155).

There has been a resurgence of interest in emotions in childhood. Saarni and Harris (1989) have edited a series of papers on children's understanding of emotion, and Garber and Dodge (1991) have edited a series of papers on the development of emotion regulation and dysregulation. But the emphasis on understanding, control, and regulation, in my view, is a reflection of the psychoanalytic view that emotions are essentially innate and that our task is to understand and control them.

Harris and Saarni (1989) recognize the work of Rosaldo (1980) and Lutz (1987) who have a perspective similar to the one that I have in this work, but then they allude to this as a radical approach to the explanation of emotional development. I agree that the approach is different, and I can only add that I have felt for some time that something different was indeed necessary.

However, consistent with the perspective that I am developing here, Sroufe (1979) and Barrett and Campos (1987) have presented an organizational and functional analysis of the ontogenesis of emotions in infancy and early childhood, and Kagan (1984) has outlined some of the changes that occur in emotions from infancy through adolescence.

Several years ago, I began a serious effort to assimilate the growing body of information about human emotions into Piaget's child development paradigm, not Piaget's cognitive development paradigm but rather his earlier paradigm in which he made observations and advanced hypotheses about both cognition and affective development, and about their relationship.

It became clear to me that Piaget wrote a number of conflicting things about the relationship between these two dimensions of development, but when I ignored the inconsistencies and studied his basic assumptions, and his approach to development as a process of construction and reconstruction always at the service of development and adaptation, then I had what I believed to be the basic tenets of a viable theory of emotional development.

In my opinion, Piaget was a consummate developmental theorist. In the Introduction to this book, I discuss why I believe Piaget lost interest in affective development. I have tried to pick up this topic where he dropped it.

The neo-Piagetian theory being advanced here is surely a product of my early interest tempered by my experience as: a school psychologist; a clinical psychologist; the director of a community mental health center; the director of a state mental health program; a professor of psychology, education, and special education; the chairperson of a university department of special education; and years of experience as a therapist for both children and adults.

My experience also included extensive work with emotionally disturbed children, some of which I reported in the literature (Dupont, Landsman, & Valentine, 1953; Dupont, 1957, 1968, 1969, 1975, 1978), over eight years of work as senior author on the development and field testing of *Toward Affective Development* (1974) and *Transition* (1979), and several efforts to articulate a theory of affective or emotional development (Dupont, 1979a, 1979b, 1989). I doubt if anyone brings more breadth of experience to the topic of emotional development than I do.

This book reflects my lifelong interest in emotional development. The theory offers an alternative to the psychoanalytic assumptions about the nature of our emotions that dominate our conventional wisdom. Freud's assumption that our emotions are instinctual and innate, and that they reside (so to speak) in our unconscious, to be understood and controlled through the process of psychoanalysis, is still a dominant notion in our conventional wisdom. If our emotions are instinctual and innate, then they have little relationship to our needs and values.

This neo-Piagetian theory of emotional development postulates that both our feelings and emotions, which are assumed to be constructions, are informed by our needs and values, and that our feelings and emotions change considerably in the course of our development. It also postulates that our consciousness is constructed as a product of our social experience, and that its acquisition plays a critical role in the development of our emotional maturity.

I sincerely believe that it is a viable theory worthy of serious consideration and research because there are important implications that flow from it.

Introduction

In his early work, Piaget was interested in both cognitive and affective development and their relationship. This interest was manifested in a number of books and papers: *Play, Dreams and Imitation in Childhood* (1951), *Six Psychological Studies* (1967), *The Psychology of the Child* (with Barbel Inhelder, 1969), *Psychology of Intelligence* (1972), and *Intelligence and Affectivity* (1981).

In most of this published material, the transformations of affect that accompany the cognitive transformations, which are central to his theory of cognitive development, are described. In *Intelligence and Affectivity* (1981, p. 14), Piaget even suggests the following stages of affective development:

Intra-individual Feelings
Hereditary organizations
First acquired feelings
Affects regulating intentional behavior

Interpersonal Feelings
Intuitive affects
Normative affects
Idealistic feelings

In all of this work, and especially in his hypothesized stages, Piaget makes it clear that he believes that affect, feelings, and emotions change in the course of development.

But then, except for two papers (invited addresses that were published in 1962 and 1976a), Piaget gave no further attention to affect and its development. He appears to have lost all interest in the topic. In fact, in an interview with Bringuier (1980) he denies ever having been interested in affect at all.

Why does he mention affect, affectivity, and even affective development in a number of works and then drop it? I believe the answer to this question is in the history of Piaget's personal development. An abbreviated chronology of Piaget's developmental history is as follows (Gruber & Vonèche, 1977, p. xli):

1896: Birth, Neuchâtel (Switzerland); first child and only son of Arthur and Rachel Piaget.

1907: First article on an albino sparrow.

1918: Doctor of Natural Sciences; thesis on molluscs, University of Neuchâtel; publication of a novel, *Recherche*.

1919-1920: Studies psychology for experimental methodology and measurement in Zürich under Lipps and Wreschner, and under Bleuler for psychiatric clinic; studies and practicum in Paris at the Alfred Binet Institute; publication of a paper on psychoanalysis.

1921: Director of studies, Jean-Jacques Rousseau Institute in Geneva; first articles on cognitive child psychology.

1923: Married Valentine Châtenay; publication of *The Language and Thought of the Child*.

1924: Publication of *Judgment and Reasoning in the Child*.

This abbreviated chronology of Piaget's developmental history suggests that his progress in his chosen field of interest was straightforward and uneventful. But there is another story, a more personal story, one that casts light on why he wrote a novel when he was but 15 years old and on why he was conflicted about studying affect.

Piaget (1952) revealed many details of his early experience in an article he wrote for a book edited by Boring, *History of Psychology in Autobiography*; in a novel he wrote when he was 15, *Recherche*; and in an interview with Anthony (1976a) in which Piaget provided the following biographical data:

At Age 7 or Earlier. Because of his mother's mental disorder (Anthony believed she was psychotic) Piaget gave up playing. He did this partly in imitation of his father, a scholar who taught him the value of systematic work and "to take refuge in a private and nonfictitious world" (p. 239).

"I have always," Piaget wrote, "detested any departure from reality, an attitude which I relate to this important influential factor of my early life, namely, my mother's poor mental state" (p. 239).

At Age 10. He became a very serious collector and classifier of molluscs and spent all of his free time on this work. By 15, he was a recognized malacologist.

At Age 15. His mother, a devout Protestant, insisted that he take formal religious instruction. Although Piaget was a Christian and a participant in Christian youth activities, his father (who considered himself a scientist) was critical of current religious beliefs and did not attend church.

Piaget, who also considered himself a scientist, was caught in the middle of this conflict between his mother and father. He wanted to please them both, but the conflict also raised an issue for him about the relationship between religion and science. Piaget tried to resolve this issue by reading everything he could find relating to it. He appears to have taken extensive notes, filling several notebooks, but he worked so frantically at this task that his own emotional health broke down and he was forced to spend a year in the mountains. We can assume, of course, that he had been sent to the mountains with orders to avoid further study and note-taking—so he wrote a novel!

This novel, *Recherche*, is obviously autobiographical because the central character, Sebastian, is a depressed young man in the midst of a religious crisis. Writing this novel seems to have been Piaget's way of confronting his crisis and to have been his therapy. The novel also reveals a remarkable acquaintance with the philosophical and scientific thought of this period. Gruber and Vonèche (1977) provide the following synopsis of Piaget's novel:

Recherche is not a novel in the usual sense of the word. It belongs to the same tradition of introspection as the works of two other Swiss writers, Rousseau and Amiel.

Recherche means both "search" and "research"; the book is a personal journal in the form of a novel, having as its sole object, like all such journals, the ego. (p. 42)

Sebastian is absorbed with "the relations between science and faith, the value of science as a theory of knowledge, the relations between science and morality, and, finally, social salvation" (p. 42). In 210 pages, Piaget describes Sebastian's struggle with these questions. Sebastian's conflict is resolved when he concludes that:

Science gives knowledge of good and of evil. It can explain everything, but it says nothing about values. It is faith that speaks of them. Faith is not knowledge, it is action. The contradiction between faith and knowledge is thus resolved. . . . Science gives the laws of the world, faith is its engine; in obeying these two forces, social salvation is the equilibrated result. (p. 43)

Anthony (1976a) believes that Piaget resolved his conflict by constructing a magnificent theoretical edifice that was comprehensive, self-contained, internally consistent, and rigorously freed from affect—an affectless monolith (p. 241).

However, somewhat later, Anthony (1976b) seems to recognize that he was perhaps a little carried away in these characterizations of Piaget's thought and theorizing: "In an earlier article the present author went so far as to caricature Piaget's approach by describing it as a 'psychology without emotion' (Anthony, 1957). In this presentation almost twenty years later, some effort will be made to modify this global and somewhat erroneous epithet" (p. 43).

Anthony continued: "Piaget has persistently maintained from his earliest writings that affect and intelligence were two distinct but complementary and inseparable aspects of behaviour, performing different but essential functions in adapting the individual to his environment, and undergoing a parallel development with corresponding stages" (p. 43).

My own belief is that having resolved his crisis and conflict, Piaget was free to think about affect and emotion and their place in development, but he resisted examining his own emotions, as suggested in the following comments he made to Anthony (1976a):

It was this disturbing factor [his mother's poor mental health] which made me intensely interested in psychoanalysis and psychopathology but at the same time blocked any desire I had to involve myself deeper in that particular direction. As a result, I have always preferred the study of normalcy and the working of the intellect to the tricks of the unconscious. (p. 239)

But what is most interesting is that in 1921 Piaget had an eight-month psychoanalysis. In an interview with Bringuier (1980), he describes having spent one hour a day, seven days a week with a female analyst who terminated her work with him because he would not accept most of her interpretations!

Piaget, then, appears to have been interested in emotion, but he was defensive about examining his own. Perhaps the most truthful thing that can be said is that he was conflicted in his interest.

Studying Piaget's work as intensively as I have has left me with the strong impression that Piaget never managed to free himself from the notion that to study feelings and emotions was tantamount to doing psychoanalysis, something he does seem to have resisted as much as he resisted being in analysis himself.

Early in his work, Piaget points out two critical issues on which he differed with Freudian thought. The first has to do with the question, are emotions present early and then transferred from one person to another without really changing (that is, is anger always anger but merely transferred from one person to another), *or* are emotions constructed and reconstructed in early relationships and throughout our life span? Is anger at 2 different than anger at 5, 10, 15, or even 30 years of age?

The second issue has to do with the conservation of affect (emotion). According to Piaget, emotions are conserved in the constructions that comprise the various emotions, that is, in the action schemes and representational level cognitive structures which provide the form and direction for our various emotions, and *not* in the unconscious as a reservoir of emotion.

Very early in his work, Piaget (1951) was critical of the Freudian concept of the unconscious as a reservoir of ideas and emotions. In postulating an unconscious, says Piaget, Freud was committing the substantialist fallacy; he was concretizing an abstraction (p. 187).

But in all that he wrote about affect (and there is more than most people realize), Piaget was clear that although we are not always conscious of our feelings and actions—that is, the phenomenon is real—the notion of an unconscious reservoir is bad science, and our emotions *are* constructions.

As a research tool, the clinical interview (which Piaget seems to have borrowed from psychiatry) could easily have been used to study children's emotions. He had a viable hypothesis: Emotions are constructions which are transformed in the course of development. But he resisted testing this hypothesis. To my knowledge he *never* talked to any children about their feelings or emotions.

Later, psychoanalysis became very popular and Piaget's criticisms of it were ignored. His ideas were also ignored, and since he did not want to be a psychoanalyst he dropped his interest in affect. In his interview with Bringuier (1980) he said he never was interested in it anyway.

In my search for a theory of emotional development, however, I came to the conclusion that Piaget's hypothesis, that emotions are constructions that contribute to the organism's equilibrium with its environment, provides the basic foundation for a theory of emotional development.

In this book then, my objectives are: (a) to build upon the theory of emotional development that I found implicit in Piaget's writings; and (b) to describe the application of this theory to assessment, education, and psychotherapy.

Emotional Development, Theory and Applications

1

A Theory of Emotional Development

With respect to the affective life, it has frequently been noted how extensively emotional equilibrium increases with age. (Piaget, 1967, p. 3)

The range of human feelings is a product of our autonomy, and the consequent need to make important decisions. Feelings guide us in those functions. (Gaylin, 1990, p. 73)

The theory of emotional development presented here has its foundation in Piaget's child development paradigm. It is a new theory, however, in that it picks up emotional development where Piaget dropped it. The theory draws heavily on Piaget's work (1951, 1962, 1967, 1971, 1972, 1976a, 1976b, 1977, 1981); on the work of Piaget and Inhelder (1969), Shotter (1975), Bruner (1983, 1990), and Lazarus (1991a, 1991b); and on the work of the social constructionists (Harré, 1986).

My interest in constructing a theory of emotional development is a product of my personal experience, my experience as a practicing psychologist, and my experience developing affective and psychological education programs. All of these experiences left me very curious about our emotions and their development. They also left me with a compelling interest in constructing a theory of emotional development because I could not find one that satisfied my curiosity.

Berk (1989) reminds us that theories are important because they: (a) tell us what to observe, (b) tell us how the products of our observations are related, (c) provide order and meaning to our research efforts, and (d) provide us with "rational guides to practical action" (p. 5). A good theory has elegance and symmetry, and it can be aesthetically satisfying, but its real value is in its power to guide our practical efforts to accomplish some important objective.

AVOIDING REDUCTIONISM AND REIFICATION

In constructing a theory of emotional development, the two scientific fallacies that I wanted to avoid were reductionism and reification.

Reductionism dominated psychology for some time. There is no better example of reductionism than the one provided by James, who, in defining an emotion, said, "our feeling of the bodily changes *is* the emotion" (Ruch & Zimbardo, 1971, p. 387). In other words, emotions are physiological patterns of change and there is a different physiological pattern of change for each of our emotions. For decades, psychologists searched in vain for these different physiological patterns. I wanted to avoid reducing emotions to lower level functions.

I also wanted to avoid the fallacy of reification, that is, the problem of turning an abstraction into a concrete existent. This occurs when emotions are treated as real things rather than as constructions. It was difficult to avoid this fallacy because I did want to talk about anger, guilt, sadness, and so forth. My preference would have been to talk about "angering," "guilting," and "saddening" but this would have been very clumsy, so I ask my reader to remember, as I keep reminding myself, that anger, guilt, and sadness are constructions—they are processes and constructions rather than real things.

When speaking of an emotion, I have in mind a number of affective reactions that have a logic in common. My objective is to construct models of emotions as mediating processes. As you will see later, the problem of reification has important implications for theory and practice.

Piaget's early work reflected an interest in both cognitive development and what he called affective development, and their interaction. In this work, Piaget provided a conceptual framework for approaching emotional development and several hypotheses about the nature of this development, but, interestingly enough, he never interviewed any children about their feelings and emotions.

CONSTRUCTION AND RECONSTRUCTION

One of Piaget's (1981) basic hypotheses was that although a few "inborn affective reactions" were present at birth, through the processes of assimilation, accommodation, and equilibration they become an elaborate repertoire of feelings and emotions that are important for both our development and the maintenance of our intrapersonal and interpersonal, or social, equilibrium (p. 14).

Consistent with the philosophy of constructionism, which guided much of Piaget's work, a group of theorists have come to the conclusion that emotions are social constructions. In support of this conclusion, Harré (1986) cites the overwhelming evidence of cultural diversity and cognitive differentiation in the emotions of mankind.

THEORY POSTULATES

The above reference to cognitive differentiation in the emotions of mankind is related to an idea advanced and discussed in some detail by Shotter. In a brilliant little book, *Images of Man in Psychological Research* (1975), Shotter pleads for a change in the way we regard the person in our research. He says we should not simply collect more and more facts about man's behavior as an object acted upon by forces outside his control; rather, we should consider man as an agent who initiates actions for which he has reasons. To understand people, he concludes, we must study their actions and their reasons for their actions (Shotter, 1975, p. 94).

Since most people's actions are made as expressions of their feelings, it would follow that to understand people's emotions we must study their reasons for their feelings and the actions through which they express their feelings. And since our emotions are social constructions, as suggested by both Piaget (1981) and the social constructionists (Harré, 1986), the changes and transformations in the development of these reasons are an important facet of emotional development.

As mentioned in the Introduction, in his early child development work Piaget was interested in behavior. He was quite emphatic in his expression of this interest.

In *The Psychology of the Child*, written with Barbel Inhelder in 1969, Piaget makes the following statement: "*The Psychology of the Child* deals with mental growth or, what amounts to the same thing, the development of behavior patterns (including consciousness) up to adolescence" (p. vii). And later, in the same volume: "When behavior is studied in its cognitive aspect, we are concerned with its structures; when behavior is considered in its affective aspect, we are concerned with its energetics (or 'economics,' as Pierre Janet used to say)" (p. 21).

This reference to behavior puts Piaget in good company because "the tenets of behaviourism dominated the field [of psychology] until perhaps the 1950s, and psychology is still often known as the science of 'behavior' rather than the science of 'mind' " (Gregory, 1987, p. 808). Behaviorism was an attempt to make psychology a natural science free of philosophical speculation. Piaget (in his work with Inhelder, 1969), of course, insisted that in his studies of mental growth he was studying how cognitive process came to provide the structure for human behavior.

It seems clear, however, that without ever mentioning it Piaget moves into what Shotter (1975) calls a human science perspective and what Bruner (1990) calls "Folk psychology [which] is a culture's account of what makes human beings tick" (p. 13). Folk psychology "deals with the nature, causes, and consequences of those intentional states—beliefs, desires, intentions, commitments—[and it] dominate[s] the transactions of everyday life" (Bruner, 1990, p. 14). It is the psychology included in the conventional wisdom, "and because it is a reflection of culture, it partakes in the culture's way of valuing as well as its way of knowing" (Bruner, 1990, p. 14).

We are concerned then, with the intentional actions of an agent-self, a self that is interacting with other selves in a system of shared meaning—a culture. This leads us to the first postulate of this neo-Piagetian theory:

1. *All of our actions are motivated by our needs and values.* In 1967, Piaget wrote:

One can say that all action . . . all movement, all thought, or all emotion—responds to a need. Neither the child nor the adult executes any external or . . . internal act unless impelled by a motive; this motive can always be translated into a need (an elementary need, an interest, a question, etc.). (p. 6)

All emotions then, are responses to a need and the need provides the motivation for the search for something to satisfy the need, and "action terminates when a need is satisfied" (Piaget, 1967, p. 7).

Long before our emotions have a well-defined cognitive structure, they are organic level auto-regulations and, later, pure action level adaptations. Whatever level is being considered, an emotion begins when some internal or external change puts the system into disequilibrium and a need is created. The emotion ends when the need is met.

Our needs move us to be interested in those things that satisfy our needs, and these interests lead to the creation of our values. Piaget (1981) described it this way: "The elementary interests found in children are linked to fundamental organic needs. They are progressively interwoven into complex systems as the child grows up. Much later they will be intellectualized and become scales of values" (p. 34). The development and function of our value system will be discussed further in Chapter 2.

2. *Feelings provide the link between our system of values and our emotions.* For all practical purposes, feelings are energy-regulating evaluations of ongoing events and, as such, they are an integral part of each of our emotions as transitional adaptations. Positive feelings find expression in positive emotional states such as joy, happiness, and contentment. Negative feelings produce negative emotions such as anger, shame, guilt, and sadness.

This process of evaluation, as manifest in feelings, is evident in our elementary adaptive reactions in that some stimuli are attended to while other stimuli are actively rejected. The role that feelings play in this process is revealed by the fact that we attribute these actions to feelings—to likes and dislikes.

In the course of development, feelings play an increasingly important role in the development of our emotions. It could be said that the development of our feelings precedes the development of our emotions.

3. *Feelings are energy-regulating evaluations.* In contemporary cognitive theories of emotion (Lazarus, 1991a, 1991b), an appraisal of some event, situation, or object is thought to be involved in the formation of each of our emotions. This appraisal can be "intuitive" or "reflective" (as suggested by Arnold, 1960) and it can be followed by numerous "reappraisals" in the course of our emotional transactions (Lazarus, 1991a, 1991b).

When the sequence of behavior we call an emotion is observed it does appear as though some act of appraisal has occurred, but when you question the person you observe making the emotional response there is no mention of an appraisal. If you ask the person to describe his or her feelings about the object (situation or event) being responded to, however, he or she can do so at once. This description always involves a value judgment—an evaluation of the object being confronted.

These evaluations become built into the logic and vocabulary of our feelings, and we construct feelings about everything. As we develop and interact with the objects that make up our world, we are constantly assigning value to these objects and this value becomes built into our representations for these objects. Then our response to these objects—how we feel about them—is automatic and no appraisal is necessary. We appraise or reevaluate objects only when our way of responding to them is not working for us. Although Arnold (1960) and Lazarus (1991a, 1991b) prefer the term "appraisal," and Barrett and Campos (1987) prefer the term "appreciation," I prefer the term "evaluation" for this very important process.

In infancy and childhood, before the development of language, our feelings are intuitive. With language, our feelings become cognized. And, finally, with the development of a self-reflective consciousness, our feelings become part of our intelligence.

The meaning events have for us does seem to be critical in the mobilization and utilization of our energy. The more significant an event is for our survival or well-being, the more energy we mobilize for use in confronting that event. This is a biological given, and it is so automatic that we are hardly aware of it. It is a basic cognitive-somatic interaction that we are only just beginning to understand.

At birth, some feelings (evaluations) appear to be wired-in in the form of life-protecting discriminations between things that are good for us and those that are harmful. But this very primitive ability to evaluate objects as well as events and situations is greatly enhanced, elaborated, differentiated, and integrated into a very functional repertoire of feelings that becomes a part of our personal-social intelligence. Our energy mobilization and utilization varies with the operation of this intelligence.

4. *Energy mobilization and utilization are different for our respective emotions.* The notion that the physical and mental manifestations of energy mobilization and utilization are a core element in our emotional behavior has a long history. It was described by Janet (1925), given credence by Guthrie (1938), and accepted by Piaget (1967, 1981) and Piaget and Inhelder (1969).

As Piaget (1951, 1981) suggests, both our intelligence (cognition) and our affect are adaptive. Then, too, he regards affect as having to do with the energetics of our behavior. Affectivity then, has to do with the mobilization and utilization of our energy.

This suggests that in the course of development we learn to modulate our energy use according to our needs. When we are making large muscle movements to accomplish heavy work, we use a great deal of energy. When faced with life-threatening danger and we need to get away quickly or to move a heavy object quickly, we are capable of tremendous feats of strength. We use a lot of energy in a short period of time.

On the other hand, when we are making small muscle movements to accomplish some delicate task, we very carefully modulate our energy output so that we are not clumsy and spoil our delicate performance. We can also change from making large muscle, threatening gestures and actions toward another person, that is, raging at that person, to making small muscle, sensitive, delicate, tender gestures and actions toward that same person. We appear to have considerable ability to modulate and modify our energy mobilization. We do not understand this ability very well but we surely have it.

Shotter (1975) reminds us that we are agents in our own processes, and that while we are born to survive, that is, to continue living, we must try to survive. Likewise, to see we must try to see and to hear we must try to hear. All of these actions, which are very important to our living and development, require intention and effort; they are not things that automatically happen to us.

Now, trying requires effort and trying presupposes intention, that is, some goal or objective is the target of our effort. But perhaps of most importance to the line of thought I am developing here is the recognition that effort requires and utilizes energy. Our utilization of energy varies with our intention and the acts we initiate to realize our intention.

Bruner (1983) has made some observations which suggest that this is a viable hypothesis. In his studies of how the mind begins, Bruner (1983) advanced some observations which can be summarized as follows:

a. Infants are extremely labile, that is, there are large variations in their internal states as measured by their heart rates, breathing, and skin conductance. These variations in state appear to be related to sensory stimulation. As their environment varies, their state varies. We might say that their state is under the control of the environment.

b. If infants are placed in an experimental room with a visual environment that is so "soft" it provides them with nothing to look at, they will typically be in tears in 30 seconds or less. With no external stimuli controlling their internal state, they fall apart.

c. At birth, however, infants have a sucking reflex, which they use to obtain nutrients vital for their survival. This means-end linkage appears to be wired-in, but within three days they can be observed to be comforting themselves by sucking. They have established a new means-end linkage or action scheme. Assimilation has occurred. A different end—comfort—has been assimilated to the sucking scheme.

d. As infants develop a larger repertoire of means-end linkages (action schemes which are adaptive) their internal states become less labile. With the elaboration of intentional behavior, infants begin to control their own states, that is, the mobilization and modulation of their energy. (pp. 148–150)

I find these observations fascinating. Before we develop action schemes, which involve the intentional use of some means to achieve a desired end, our energy variance is under the control of our environment. But as we construct more and more action schemes and increasingly intend to realize desired ends, our internal states, our arousal, our energy variance—our emotions, if you wish—are increasingly under our control.

There is, then, a shifting of energy as our feelings change. For anger, which is actually a whole family of emotions, the amount of energy mobilized varies with the degree of threat one believes to exist in the situation being confronted. In annoyance and irritation, little energy is mobilized, but in rage and fury the energy mobilized is considerable, so much, in fact, that sometimes the energy itself becomes a problem. In sadness and guilt, there is a depression of energy, as if one is saving energy to manage the difficulty of living with the loss of a loved one or of coping with failure, or as part of being properly apologetic when one feels guilty.

This shifting in the amount of energy that one is mobilizing and using frequently involves bodily changes, such as changes in heartbeat and breathing, and sometimes even changes in body chemistry (as, for example, when adrenaline kicks in when one is severely frightened or enraged). There also appear to be changes in posture and facial expression that are correlated with different feelings and emotions.

In the emotions requiring an action to complete them, energy is required to support the action, so typically there is a considerable shift in the amount of energy being mobilized and used. Feelings are another matter; they require little energy since they are just an evaluation, a cognitive operation.

However, because our feelings and emotions were originally an undifferentiated response, feelings include a residual tendency to act in some adaptive way. These impulses to action are the remnants of our elementary wired-in adaptive affective reactions, which, at birth, were essential to our survival.

With development, and the need for delay and flexibility in our reactions, these impulses are increasingly brought under cognitive control. Feelings and emotions become two functionally different constructions; feelings become energy-regulating evaluations and emotions become actions, informed by feelings, that restore our equilibrium.

5. *With development, emotions become cognitive constructions with a distinctive structure or logic for each emotion.* As early as 2 or 3 years of age, many children can describe reasons for both their feelings and the actions through which they "express" their feelings. These reasons constitute a kind of logic of relationships which, in the course of development, becomes a distinctive logic for each human emotion.

Although Piaget (1981) did not stress the logic inherent in our emotions as cognitive constructions, he acknowledged that such a logic might exist and that social factors could play a role in its construction: "Conservation of values . . . implies a logic of feelings" (p. 60) and "the uniformity and consistency of expression enforced by social life plays a large part, therefore, in the development of intellectual structures with their conservations and invariants; and it will lead to analogous transformations in the domain of feelings" (p. 60).

When I first encountered empirical evidence of this idea in the interview data I had from children 5, 10, and 15 years of age, I did not know what to make of it. The notion that, with development, each of our emotions would become a cognitive construction shaped by social considerations and be similar from one person to the next was simply astonishing to me. But some data I had on children's constructions for jealousy shows this rather convincingly.

The data were obtained through a projective procedure in which children were shown a picture of a child with a facial expression exhibiting jealousy, told that the child was jealous, and then asked, "Why does this child feel jealous?" and "What will happen next?"

Responses were obtained from twenty males and twenty females at 5, 10, and 15 years of age. Each child's response was typed on an index card and the cards were then grouped according to the reasons (the objects) the children gave for the feeling and the action they described as following the feeling.

The responses made by the 5-year-old children are shown in Table 1.

As revealed in their reasons for feeling jealous, only two (5%) of these children had acquired the logic of jealousy, ten (25%) were

Table 1
The Development of 5-Year-Old Children's Constructions for Jealousy

Construction	Object	Number	Frequency
Jealous	Someone took friend away	1	
Jealous	Parent holding another child	$\dfrac{1}{2}$	.05
Envious	Doesn't have what other has	10	.25
Angry or Sad	Doesn't have or can't do something	2	
Angry	Doesn't like other child	2	
Angry	Is mad at or frustrated	$\dfrac{3}{7}$	.17
Angry	Didn't know or gave unclassifiable response	21	.53

N = 40

not differentiating between envy and jealousy, seven (17%) had only the logic of anger or sadness, and twenty-one (53%), or over half of them, did not know what jealousy was.

The responses made by the 10-year-old children are shown in Table 2.

As revealed in their reasons for feeling jealous, nineteen (46%) of these children had acquired the logic of jealousy, eighteen (45%) offered the logic of envy, and four (9%) offered reasons that are typically given for either anger or sadness by most children this age.

The responses made by the 15-year-old children are shown in Table 3.

Table 2
The Development of 10-Year-Old Children's Constructions for Jealousy

Construction	Object	Number	Frequency
Jealous	Friend giving attention to or playing with other; other is taking friend	15	
Jealous	Parent is giving attention to sibling	4 ___ 19	.46
Envious	Other has something they want or is doing something they want to do	18	.45
Angry or Sad	Can't do, couldn't do something wanted to do	4	.09
N = 40 (One child gave alternate responses.)			

As revealed in their reasons for feeling jealous, thirty-two (80%) of these children had acquired the logic of jealousy and eight (20%) offered the logic of envy. None of these 15-year-old children were failing to differentiate between anger and jealousy.

This age-related convergence toward a socially shared logic for feeling jealous illustrates the process that I believe is at work in the development of all of our feelings, and our emotions as well.

By what actions do children turn feeling jealous into the emotion of jealousy? As postulated in my theory, the actions children suggest should restore their sense of well-being (their equilibrium). What actions do these children at 5, 10, and 15 years of age suggest? My data are most interesting.

Only two of the 5-year-old children had jealousy constructions. One child suggested that the child in the picture would be jealous because "somebody took her friend away," but then she insisted that she did not know what would happen next. Another child said

Table 3
The Development of 15-Year-Old Children's Constructions for Jealousy

Construction	Object	Number	Frequency
Jealous	Other is getting friend's attention or friend is giving attention to other	32	.80
Envious	Other has something he or she wants or better than he or she has	8	.20
N = 40			

that she would feel jealous because "her mother is holding the baby and she wants to be held." When asked what would happen next, she responded, "Then she'll be feeling happy because then her mother always holds her." Interestingly enough, the only two 5-year-old children who had acquired the logic of feeling jealous were female.

Nineteen of the 10-year-old children had acquired the logic of feeling jealous. Of these, four involved having siblings that were getting something from their parents that they did not get. Two of these children said they would ask their parents to give them what the siblings got, one suggested doing things to attract the parents' attention, and one said she would just forget about it.

Fifteen of the 10-year-old children's responses involved the familiar jealousy triangle. Another person likes, gives attention to, or takes away a "good" friend, or the "good" friend gives attention to another person, sometimes another friend. Three of the children reported a kind of magical improvement in the situation; for example, "Her boyfriend could go back to her." Two suggested that she could "just walk off" or "start crying."

Ten (25%) of these children, however, suggested some action directed toward their "good" friend or toward the other person; for example, "She'll be mad at him and won't talk to him," or "Probably take one of that girl's friends away." All of the actions of twenty-five percent of the 10-year-old children were some variation of these two actions; none of these actions appear to be very effective. No gender differences were evident.

These two kinds of actions were also suggested by the 15-year-old children. Fifteen (38%) would "fight with" the "good" friend, "try to make the ["good"] friend jealous," or "get mad at" and "not speak to" the "good" friend, but ten (25%) would "fuss at," "be mad at," or "take it out" on the other person, and two would "give up" or "pout." There were only two actions that I would consider to be effective: "Talking with the ["good"] friend" (suggested by one child) or "Trying harder with the ["good"] friend" (suggested by two children).

Left to themselves, children ages 5, 10, and 15 do not appear to be constructing very effective ways of dealing with the situations in which they feel jealous. By age 15, eighty percent of them have acquired socially appropriate reasons for (or the logic of) feeling jealous but the actions they have in mind do not make jealousy a very adaptive emotion.

Although we asked children why they felt jealous and what would happen next, I wish that we had also asked them *why* they suggested that action as a way of acting upon the feeling. Their answers to this question would have provided us with the logic of both the feeling and the emotion. It would have increased considerably our understanding of their emotional development.

Let us put aside for the moment our concern about how ineffective jealousy is for these children and focus on another aspect of what I am suggesting here. Let me call your attention to my notion that these children are in the process of acquiring (or constructing) a socially sanctioned logic of jealousy as a feeling (an energy-regulating evaluation) and then as an emotion (an action upon the feeling).

Why am I stressing the idea of children acquiring or constructing the logic of jealousy? Why am I not talking about children learning to recognize or understand feeling jealous? The answer to these two questions is critical to my whole conception (my theory) of emotional development.

First, feelings and emotions are not things to be recognized or understood as if they are real things, like plants or trees or even animals, which have biochemical or physiological processes to be discovered and whose meaning can be understood as biochemical or physiological processes. Second, feelings and emotions are personal constructions whose meaning is to be understood within the context of the socially shared meaning (or culture) in which they are constructed. They are not *discovered*. They are *constructed*. Their logic is acquired as the child becomes a human being in a culture created by other human beings. I believe the interview data I have just presented on jealousy illustrates this phenomenon very well.

Jealousy is a form of anger. It is a reaction to events and situations that people evaluate as being a threat to their well-being, typically an event or situation in which someone they feel close to is showing attention or affection to another, or another is showing attention or affection to someone they feel close to. But this linkage or logic becomes constructed through their social experience and it is an elaboration of, or transformation of, the more simple logic of anger and envy. Only two children at 5 years of age had acquired this logic, but nineteen children at 10 years of age and thirty-two children at 15 years of age had acquired it, although even at age 15 it does not appear to have become a very effective emotion. Why this is true is not clear.

The logic of jealousy then, is not something that is discovered; it is, rather, something that is acquired or constructed by persons in their social relationships within a context of socially shared meaning. Jealousy is acquired late in most children's development. Its construction depends upon the child's social experience and cognitive development.

These same factors are involved in the construction of all of our emotions. For many feelings and emotions, the cognitive development and social experience necessary for their development occurs much earlier. This is certainly true for anger, shame, sadness, pride, and happiness. Guilt, like jealousy, is acquired somewhat later.

The construction of each feeling and emotion depends upon the acquisition of a particular self-in-relationship-with-others conception or logic. These constructions are the product of our cognitive development and our social experience.

These core conceptions, which will be discussed more fully in Chapter 3, are shown in Table 4.

What is involved here is this. In order to feel angry people must be able to conceive of themselves as being threatened unfairly. In

Table 4
Core Conceptions for Feeling Angry, Ashamed, Guilty, Sad, Proud, or Happy

Feeling	Conception
Angry	Threats to one's well-being or identity that are considered unfair
Ashamed	Being inferior or flawed
Guilty	Having done wrong or harmed others
Sad	Having lost significant other or failed in a significant way
Proud	Accomplishing something or having a valued identity
Happy	Being well and doing well

order to feel ashamed people must be able to conceive of themselves as being inferior or flawed. In order to feel guilty people must be able to conceive of themselves as having done wrong or as having harmed others. In order to feel sad people must have a conception of loss and failure. In order to feel proud people must have a conception of achieving in spite of obstacles. And in order to feel happy people must have a conception of being well and doing well. As we shall see, these conceptions (presented in a highly abstract form here) undergo considerable transformation in the course of development.

As constructions built around these core conceptions, our emotions mediate all of our transactions with our social world. Moved by our needs and values, as manifested in our feelings, we initiate actions to restore our equilibrium. These actions are provided a pattern or structure by our imagery and thought, and constitute a distinctive logic for each of our emotions.

The above is a good description of what happens with our negative feelings for, in effect, they constitute a problem to be solved. We feel threatened, we feel ashamed, we feel guilty, or we feel sad. Each of these feelings is a response to an event or situation that must be managed or dealt with in some constructive way, so we initiate some action to deal with it.

Our positive emotions are not quite that simple. They are more affective states that follow some action by others or by ourselves that we evaluate as positive or beneficial for our well-being or our identity. I base this conclusion on my study of pride and happiness.

Younger children attribute pride and happiness to things that significant others do for them, but older children feel proud or happy when they can evaluate their own goal-directed behavior and their consciousness as positive and beneficial, as something to be enjoyed or even celebrated. They feel happy when they are doing well and all is going well.

Somewhere in the course of development, probably around 10 to 13 years of age, the logic of pride and happiness changes from significant others to the self as the "cause" of the feeling. This will be discussed in more detail in Chapter 3.

6. *Emotions are constructed in discourse with others.* Although a few elementary feelings and emotions appear to be wired-in at birth, with development, and especially with the development of language and consciousness, they become elaborated into an extensive repertoire of feelings and emotions that contribute to our equilibrium.

Let me be clear at this point about how radical a notion it is that our feelings and emotions are a product of construction—that they *are* constructions. The conventional wisdom has been so strongly influenced by psychoanalytic theory that it is simply assumed that all of our emotions are innate.

According to Freudian theory, these feelings and emotions, present at birth, are invested in the objects that make up the infant's world (parents, for example) and are then transferred to other objects as they come into the child's world. Anger and joy, for example, are the same at maturity as they are in infancy; they are just invested in different objects.

Piaget (1981) suggests an alternative hypothesis. A few elementary feelings and emotions are present at birth, but in the course of development they become elaborated and differentiated through the processes of assimilation and accommodation into new constructions, that is, new feelings and emotions. And rather than simply being transferred from one person to another, anger and joy (again as examples) are transformed in the course of development so that, at maturity, they are quite different than in early childhood. Barrett and Campos (1987) have a similar position on this issue: "We clearly do not believe that emotions remain unchanged during the course of development" (p. 567).

Kagan (1984) also shares this position: "The popular belief that a child's emotions do not change with growth requires the improbable assumption that maturational changes in the brain that produce new cognitive evaluations and special feeling tones have no influence on the older person's emotional experiences" (p. 172).

The importance of this issue is reflected in some recent work on early emotional development by Dunn and Brown (1991). Although most of the research on children 2 to 3 years of age has focused narrowly on the function of attachment, Dunn and Brown report on three longitudinal studies they conducted on relationships, talk about feelings, and affect regulation in early childhood. Their studies involved home observation and the tape-recorded family discourse of six families (forty-three children) and then a second set of six families.

Dunn and Brown (1991) discuss their findings relating to affective states within the context of Stern's persuasive argument that the acquisition of language enables children to participate in "shared meanings," which transforms children's relationships so that "being with" others is now possible. "With their ability to use language, children take a major step in separation and individuation, but also, Stern maintained, a step in emotional relatedness, as they are able to negotiate shared meanings" (p. 90).

In the discussion of their observations and conclusions about what is ostensibly affective regulation, Dunn and Brown (1991) refer repeatedly to children's developing influence over their own affective states. In a review of their own research and the selected research of others, Dunn and Brown (1991) found convincing evidence for the following:

a. During the second and third years of their lives, children's "ability to explain their own [affective] state and enlist comfort or aid and to achieve their own emotional ends by persuading others or by deceiving them about their own state increases dramatically" (p. 91). Children become especially adept at soliciting the aid of others to alleviate their distress or discomfort.

b. During this same period, children begin to use references to the affective states and likes and dislikes of others to achieve their own desires. They also begin to express concern for others' affective states.

c. The ability to talk about feelings and their causes enables children "to express their affection and to ask for and receive affection" (p. 92).

d. "Just as children communicate their need to alleviate their negative feelings, they also frequently draw attention to their successes and pleasures" (p. 93).

e. During the second and third years, children's increasing ability to understand and influence others' "affective states is evident in a range of different actions . . . [such as] comforting others, teasing, and joking" (p. 97). These efforts show the "pleasure the children experience in sharing their positive affect with particular others and their ability to manipulate effectively the emotions of another—again, to their own satisfaction" (p. 101).

f. "With the ability to share humor, to amuse others, to tease, to express their concern in successful comforting, children achieve a new intimacy in their relationships and a new way of expressing themselves in those relationships" (p. 101).

What permitted or facilitated these dramatic changes or transformations? Dunn and Brown (1991) believe that four things were involved: (a) during this age period children observe the facial expressions, actions, and verbalizations of others; (b) they engage in pretend play where their own affective states and the affective states of others are often the central topic of their play; (c) they comment on their own affective states and they ask their mothers direct questions about others' affective states (many mothers responded to these comments and questions most of the time; some, unfortunately did not); and (d) they have affective exchanges with siblings.

They also found evidence for large individual differences in child-parent discourse. Some mothers did not respond to their children's comments and questions as frequently as other mothers did. These differences were correlated with the children's affective perspective-taking abilities one year later and again, three years later, in middle childhood.

This work reviewed by Dunn and Brown (1991) is brilliant and ground-breaking. It shows, in bold relief, the limitations of the conventional wisdom that feelings and emotions are innate so that our major challenge is learning how to regulate or control their expression. They indicate their discomfort with this conception early in their review:

But if we include in our notion of "affect regulation" children's interactions with others—that is, if we see affect regulation not simply as a private "homeostatic" mechanism but also as a feature of children's relationships with others—then this period of the second and third year must be highlighted even more as one of the major developmental changes in children's control and influence over their emotional states. (Dunn & Brown, 1991, p. 89)

However, they cannot seem to break free of the idea that our feelings and emotions just evolve to be controlled and influenced. I suggest that in these children's exchanges with their parents and siblings (in which affective states and their causes and effects were observed, commented on, their causes questioned, probably labeled, and then explored in pretend play) that their own affective states were transformed into the need- and value-informed cognitive constructions we call our feelings and emotions.

It is my belief, then, that feelings and emotions are constructed in these social relationships and in exchanges with others. They are not just controlled or influenced—they are constructed. I am reminded here of Shotter's (1975) words: "Before anything becomes a mental function proper [a feeling or emotion] . . . it must first exist externally, as an exchange between two people. We become ourselves through others. And the reasons why we become what we are can be found 'out there' in the world, rather than deep within our private, inner workings" (p. 101).

As you will see, the notion that emotions are constructions has many very important implications for emotional development; in fact, this assumption is a basic one for the very idea that a theory of emotional development is possible at all.

7. *There is both transformation and conservation in the construction of our feelings and emotions.* There is evidence that some of our feelings and emotions are transformed in the course of development. In the discussion of Postulate 5, I identified six core well-be-

ing (and/or identity) conceptions in the logic of four negative and two positive feelings and emotions. These conceptions appear in the abstract to be central to these six feelings and emotions at all age levels.

However, there are transformations in the logic of the feelings and the actions through which the feelings are expressed that are age-related. These transformations are reviewed in some detail in Chapter 3.

There is also evidence that other emotions are constructed and that some are deconstructed in the course of development. Let me consider this question within the context of another basic consideration.

Are basic affects present early, there to be built upon for the rest of our development, or are there only affective reactions as constructions, always with two elements, one structured and the other motivational (value-related)? And are these affective reactions created to be either conserved or to disappear when they are no longer needed? For example, do not whining, pouting, and some kinds of crying (raging) disappear as affective reactions for most people?

I suspect that there are other affective reactions that also come and go. Some may never be named; they are constructed when they are needed and their structure may be only in their action pattern, or in some imagery or perhaps as a scene remembered whole, as suggested by Kaufman (1992, pp. 192–195). They are constructed because they are needed for the child's adaptation; they help the child create and maintain a basic constancy and continuity that may be essential for his or her well-being.

Indeed, some children who live in worlds that are very different require very different constructions to ensure their survival and development. With a change in their situation new constructions are necessary, but new constructions take time. There is, at first, the effort to assimilate the new to the old. There may be a period of serious disequilibrium and then an accommodation. The higher the individual's level of cognitive development, the easier the reequilibration process may be. There can be a planned change rather than just a groping and stumbling change.

As suggested earlier, some feelings and emotions are conserved, first in action patterns and then in cognitions, only to be transformed in the course of development (Piaget, 1951, pp. 187–189).

But which ones? The answer to this question is both simple and complex.

We conserve and transform those feelings and emotions that serve our adaptation—those that involve personally and socially significant well-being and identity issues (that is, those sanctioned by our culture). But (as we will see) as our needs and values change, our way of construing these issues changes and so does our response to them.

8. *Social experience is critical for the development of self-reflective consciousness and for emotional development.* Consciousness, cognition, and emotions are all transformed through construction and reconstruction in the course of development. Piaget and Inhelder (1969) attributed development to four factors: (a) maturation, (b) physical experience, (c) social experience and feedback, and (d) self-regulation, making social experience an indispensable factor in development.

Our intelligence and our consciousness, then, are essential for our emotional development. At maturity, we are conscious of and clear about our feelings and conscious of the logic of our choice of action upon our feelings. And, at the highest levels of equilibrium (social equilibrium) we must also be conscious of how others are reacting to our emotional actions, and the probable consequences of our actions or any new actions that we might initiate.

What this suggests to me is simply this. We cannot achieve the level of self-reflective consciousness without social experience. We cannot do it alone. We are dependent on the discourse and, eventually, the dialogue we have with others to achieve this highest level of consciousness. The transformation of our conceptualization of what we are doing and why, which is central to our consciousness, requires that we talk about our feelings and choice of actions (our emotions) with others.

But that "talk" must be a dialogue in which there is a real exchange of perspectives and ideas. There must be questions that challenge others' reasons for their feelings and their reasons for the actions they chose as ways of acting upon their feelings, that is, their reasons for the actions they initiated to manage the various events and situations that are the objects of their feelings.

9. *Self-reflective consciousness is essential for the achievement of the highest levels of equilibrium.* Earlier, I described emotions as per-

sonal-social constructions, emphasizing that there is always a person (a self) that is constructing the emotion, albeit within a social context. If our emotions mediate our social interactions, then to be self-regulating at the highest levels of equilibrium we must be conscious of how others are reacting to our emotional actions. This makes consciousness a critical variable in our self-regulation, which is important not only for our minute-to-minute well-being but for our emotional development as well (Piaget & Inhelder, 1969, p. 157).

Piaget (1951) was critical of Freud's theory of consciousness. In creating the unconscious as a compartment of the mind, Piaget believed that Freud was committing the substantialist fallacy. The phenomenon is real, said Piaget, but not Freud's explanation of it. To avoid the substantialist fallacy, consciousness must be regarded as a series of reactions and not as repressed memories (p. 187).

Later, Piaget (1976b) studied consciousness and discovered that consciousness was constructed in the course of development in parallel with cognition and affectivity. As was typical of Piaget, he studied the development of children's consciousness of their impersonal problem-solving activities, then suggested that his conclusions must also apply to the affective domain.

Piaget concluded that consciousness involves the development of a language for the events we are attending to (we cognize the events and their various elements; we symbolize them and represent them in thought) and then we integrate them conceptually (we include them in our understanding of how things work; we develop a psychology for these events).

Piaget (1976b) also concluded that there are at least four levels of consciousness that are significant for the kinds of self-regulation they make possible: (a) organic level auto-regulation, (b) the self-regulation of actions without conceptualization, (c) the self-regulation of actions with concrete level conceptualization, and (d) a reflective level of self-regulation with abstract conceptualization.

10. *Emotional maturity is having a rich repertoire of feelings and emotions, and a self-reflective consciousness (or understanding) of how they work for us.* Emotional maturity is not just being super-rational and replacing emotion with reason. Reason alone can take us to terrible conclusions like the "final solution" that led to The Holo-

caust. No! Reason and feelings and emotions informed by our values are essential to a fully human emotional maturity.

Emotional maturity also involves the construction of a psychology that is a personal version of the folk psychology that is our cultural inheritance. In a system of shared meaning—a culture—people develop a system of values and a system of personal meaning that includes a theory about what makes life work.

Piaget (1967) didn't quite say this, but he did describe how:

> Personality formation begins in middle to late childhood (eight to twelve years) with the autonomous organization of rules and values, and the affirmation of will with respect to the regulation and hierarchical organization of moral tendencies. . . . There is then a "personal" system in the dual sense that it is peculiar to a given individual and implies autonomous coordination. Now this personal system cannot be constructed prior to adolescence, because it presupposes the formal thought and reflexive constructions we have just discussed [thought and its operations]. (p. 65)

Bruner (1990), concerned that the cognitive revolution in psychology had been diverted by the "computational metaphor," urges us to return to our concern for "*meaning* and the processes and transactions involved in the construction of meanings" (p. 33). He offers a twofold argument for this action: "The first is that to understand man you must understand how his experiences and his acts are shaped by his intentional states, and the second is that the form of these intentional states is realized only through participation in the symbolic systems of the culture" (Bruner, 1990, p. 33).

What this suggests to me is that emotional maturity requires us to develop a personal psychology that is congruent with the folk psychology of our culture. Indeed, our personal psychology has meaning only within the context of our culture's folk psychology. As you will see, this way of thinking about emotional maturity has important implications for education and psychotherapy.

——— 2 ———

Needs, Values, Feelings, and Emotions

We have seen that human behaviour is characterised by a high internal delay in preparation for deferred action. The biological groundwork for this inaction stretches through the long childhood and slow maturation of man. But deferment of action in man goes far beyond that. Our actions as adults, as decision makers, as human beings, are mediated by values, which I interpret as general strategies in which we balance opposing impulses. It is not true that we run our lives by any computer scheme of problem solving. The problems of life are insoluble in this sense. Instead, we shape our conduct by finding principles to guide it. We devise ethical strategies or systems of values to ensure that what is attractive in the short term is weighed in the balance of the ultimate, long-term satisfactions. (Bronowski, 1973, p. 436)

ON THE NATURE OF NEEDS AND VALUES

In Postulates 1 and 2 of this theory of emotional development, I advanced the idea that all of our actions are motivated by our needs and values and that feelings provide the link between our system of values and our emotions.

Both Piaget (1981) and Branden (1969) were convinced that there is a causal linkage between our values and our feelings and emotions. Piaget (1981) put it this way: "As values are accorded to actions and to other people, they come to play a considerable role in the subsequent development of feelings" (p. 42). Branden (1969) was somewhat more emphatic: "The relationship of value-judgments to emotions is that of *cause* to *effect*. An emotion is a value-response. It is the automatic psychological result (involving both mental and somatic features) of a super-rapid, subconscious appraisal" (pp. 68–69).

Hobson (1985) was also confident about the relationship between values and feelings: "Feeling is a voluntary process. It is a valuing. . . . Feeling imparts a *value* to experiences and involves a choice mediated by like and dislike, approval and disapproval, acceptance and rejection, approach and avoidance. It involves a *judgement*" (p. 90).

Piaget, Branden, and Hobson, then, gave value and valuing a very important role in our feelings and emotions. But how are values acquired? There is a rather general acceptance of the idea that our values are linked to our needs, but just how this linkage is established is not clear.

Consistent with his Freudian background, Maslow (1971) believed that our needs are biologically based and intrinsic in nature:

I believe I make a good case for accepting the probable instinctoid character of one's highest values, i.e., of what might be called the spiritual or philosophical life. Even this personally discovered axiology I feel can be subsumed under this category of "phenomenology of one's own instinctoid nature" or of "subjective biology" or "experiential biology" or some such phrase. (p. 32)

Maslow was almost mystical about the relationship between needs and values. He will be describing or discussing needs at some length and then begin referring to them as values, and his list of needs and values is rather long. In addition to what Maslow (1971) calls survival needs—the physiological and safety needs—there are the basic needs of belongingness, affection, respect, and self-esteem, and then fifteen self-actualizing needs that he calls "Being-Values" (pp. 318–319).

But Piaget had a very different conception of instincts. He believed that there are only three instinctual or "fundamental needs of food, protection against enemies, and reproduction"

(Piaget, 1971, p. 349) and that our instincts are always at the service of these needs. However, he went on to say that with our evolution as a species, instincts as hereditary programs have been replaced by intelligence or "constructive autoregulation" (Piaget, 1971, p. 366).

So we have conflicting views on the nature of our needs and values. Maslow (1971), in the Freudian tradition, said that all of them—our elementary, basic, and Being-Values—are instinctual in nature. Piaget (1981) said there are only three fundamental needs but that we do develop a system of values and some of them ("children's interests") are linked to "organic needs" (p. 34). Piaget's fundamental needs for food, protection, and reproduction are comparable to Maslow's physiological and safety needs, but all agreement seems to end there.

There is yet another very basic difference in the beliefs of Piaget and Maslow. As mentioned earlier, Piaget believed that every disequilibrium we experience creates a need that must be satisfied. This means that our needs, far from being instinctive, are the product of our interactions with our environment. Maslow believed that our needs and values are the expression of our inner nature.

Maslow's notion that values are instinctive and thus "inner" in origin is disputed by Vygotsky as noted by Shotter (1975), who paraphrases Vygotsky in these words: "Before anything becomes a mental function proper located 'within' an individual, it must first exist externally, as an exchange between two people. . . . The reasons why we become what we are can be found 'out there' in the world, rather than deep within our private inner workings" (p. 101).

This is close to the position expressed by Rokeach (1973) who said that our values also reflect the demands of our culture:

Values are the cognitive representation not only of individual needs but also of societal and institutional demands. They are the joint results of sociological as well as psychological forces acting upon the individual—sociological because society and its institutions socialize the individual for the common good to internalize shared conceptions of the desirable; psychological because individual motivations require cognitive expression, justification, and indeed exhortation in socially desirable terms. The cognitive representation of needs as values serves societal demands no less than individual needs. (p. 20)

Piaget sees values as "linked" to needs whereas Rokeach sees them as representations of needs. I am more inclined to accept Piaget's position that there is a linkage rather than a one-to-one relationship between needs and values, but I am also inclined to accept Rokeach's suggestion that values reflect society's demands and injunctions. I believe that our values *are* part of the meaning we share in our culture.

Piaget (1981) expressed a preference for Lewin's field theory as an explanation for how values are created and how they influence our actions (pp. 34–35). In everyday language, Lewin's field theory suggests the following.

In the process of meeting our needs, both the actions and actual objects that meet our needs acquire value which we experience as a valence that can be either positive or negative. We have a number of needs and the actions and objects involved in meeting our needs take on valence.

These valences then operate as a value grid in our consciousness. With development, they become an organized system of values which is given representation in our feelings. The element of value arises in the interaction between individuals and objects within a cultural context of shared meaning. But once an object acquires value, we act as if the value is located in the object.

Maslow (1971) suggested that our needs and values are hierarchical in nature—lower needs must be met before higher needs can be attended to. My intuition suggests something different. There is an element of increasing cognitive complexity and abstraction to our consciousness, which includes our needs and values. Rather than meeting each need in turn, it is more likely that our needs are and remain an organizing and energy-regulating element in our field of consciousness, and they are not so much met as they are taken into account. Let me try to illustrate what I have in mind here.

An infant kicks off her blanket and becomes cold. She is uncomfortable. She cries. A caretaker comes and puts the blanket back, taking care to tuck the infant into the blanket. The child's hand grasps the blanket for the first time, making her aware of it. The blanket and her comfort become linked together for her. She values the blanket. The need involved here is comfort and, as a result of this sequence at the pure action level, the blanket becomes invested with value. The next time the child is uncomfortable, she will search for the blanket.

The child's need for comfort, however, is meaningful only within the context of her need for constancy. It was the change in body temperature that made the child uncomfortable. Her need for constancy and comfort were organizing her field of consciousness.

As needs are met then, they don't cease to exist; they are still there as background for whatever need is in the foreground. As we mature and have new social experiences, new needs arise and then they reorganize the field. Earlier needs don't cease to exist; they remain as part of the landscape (so to speak) but they are now part of the background, and the field is a new field with the new need now in the foreground.

The function of needs and how they create values may be easier to see when other needs are involved—for example, competence. Early in children's lives, even before they are in school, competency is probably important. Children feel compelled to finish what they have started, then to do it according to some imagery they have for the task, which they have probably gotten from watching someone else. Eventually, they do it well and they experience considerable satisfaction. Doing it well then, is something they value for the rest of their lives, and they develop certain habits that make it highly probable that most things that they do will be done well. Then they value these habits, so they keep meeting the need for competency but it is now background and some other need becomes foreground.

What if a need is poorly attended to? It may remain in the foreground and influence the assimilation of all subsequent needs and, therefore, the organization of the field. As I have suggested, some of our needs are psychosocial in nature and they pull us more than they push us. They pull our attention because they are there in the field we are confronting and we must take them into account. I believe that our actions reflect our values, and that what we value reflects our needs.

During the course of emotional development, our field of consciousness is essentially a cognized value grid that controls our energy output, and it is a configuration of all of the needs we are confronting at that time. A need is not simply met and then forgotten; it continues to be in the field contributing to the configuration of the field so that, at maturity, we are meeting all of those needs of which we have some consciousness.

There are large-scale individual differences in the systems of values we develop. Some people develop a system of values that is simple, concrete, and crude; others develop a system of values that is complex, abstract, and very sensitive to subtle differences. Since I believe that feelings are best regarded as energy-regulating evaluations, you can simply substitute the word "feelings" for the word "values" in the above statement and the meaning is the same. Gaylin (1979) has written something that is similar to what I am saying here:

Feelings, therefore, particularly the complex and subtle range of feelings in human beings, are testament to our capacity for choice and learning. Feelings are the instrument of rationality, not as some would have it—alternatives to it. Because we are intelligent creatures—meaning that we are freed from instinctive and patterned behavior to a degree unparalleled in the animal kingdom—we are capable of, and dependent on, using rational choice to decide our futures. (p. 7)

I would add to this that our rational choice is a rational, *value-informed* choice, and that freeing ourselves from action patterns of which we are not conscious is one of the things emotional development is all about.

A WORKING LIST

With all of this in mind, I searched my case material and especially the interview data that I had collected over the years (some of which was data shared by several colleagues) for evidence of needs and values. The list of needs and values presented below is the product of that search:

Basic
Constancy
Comfort
Being valued and cared for

Psychological
Play
Novelty
Connections and relationships
Competence
Competition
Achievement
Self-esteem

Psychosocial
Identity
Mutuality
Autonomy
Integrity

Spiritual
A faith to live by

I offer this list with some trepidation. Please consider it a work in progress. I have, however, found it useful.

There is one thing about this list that is quite unusual. Notice that I call it a list of needs *and* values. Almost all of the entries on this list are both, but at the lower end of the list the entries are more consistently needs that generate values as they are met. But at the highest level the needs, themselves, do become values. I think this follows from the fact that, with development, our consciousness becomes more complex and abstract.

DISCUSSION

I would now like to discuss each of these needs and values as I understand them:

Constancy. We appear to need a certain constancy and continuity in our experience, so we abhor interruptions and distractions. We appear to have a need to finish what we have started. This need appears to lead to a valuing of having at least some control over our stimulation, our involvement, and our experience.

Comfort. This appears to be another basic need. Many changes make us uncomfortable and a number of deprivations cause us pain and discomfort. Interestingly enough, we can also be uncomfortable when satiated. Stimulation that is too intense can be painful and uncomfortable. Injury and illness make us uncomfortable. We value those things that are linked to our comfort.

Being valued and cared for. There is little doubt that we need care, and we seem to thrive when we are valued. Some would call this love; others may prefer to call this empathy. We need the feeling that someone cares about and understands us. Some people go to great lengths to create this feeling, and it is a lifelong value.

Play. All animals and children need to play but so do adults, that is, to just do a number of things for the simple pleasure of doing them. We value the implements and equipment that we use in our play and the opportunity to play. The form this need takes and the values linked to it change in the course of development but it is a lifelong and universal need.

Novelty. We appear to need novelty. Although this need would appear to be in conflict with constancy it is not. Actually, it is against a background of constancy that novelty is meaningful. We express this need when we say, "Let's do something different for a change," or "Let's try that this time." In a world of sameness, we are attracted to the novel or different. It, too, can be a lifelong need and lead us to value novel things and novel experiences.

Connections and relationships. This need appears early and it is also a lifelong need. We need relationships of all kinds. Children will express the need to have others to play with, but later they want friends, then partners, and later, to belong to some group. This need is met by having a peer group of friends, that is, a clique or a gang.

Some psychologists believe that connection is a deeply rooted need for women. Whether this is biological or social in origin is not an issue here. The important thing is that connections and relationships appear to be more highly valued by females than by males. This difference in values appears relatively early in my data.

This need-value is also being given considerable attention by female psychologists interested in female development. Gilligan, Lyons, and Hanmer (1990), and Jordan, Kaplan, Miller, Stiver, and Surrey (1991) have studied the need for connection in some detail. And Jordan (1993) puts it this way: "A relational perspective on human experience suggests that we grow in , through, and toward relationship; for women especially, connections with others are central to psychological well-being."

Men also appear to value relationships, but the extent to which relationships are valued appears, for many, to be overridden by other concerns.

These apparent differences and what follows from them have important implications for education and psychotherapy. Surely this entire issue deserves continued study.

Competence. Very early in our development we seem to have a need to feel competent, which appears to include the notion that we have mastery in some area of skill, performance, or understanding. "I can do that," "I know that," or "I did it right" appears early in children's self-reports.

Both genders express this need in early childhood, and males continue to need and value evidence of their competence. My impression is that in the course of development it becomes less of a value for females.

Men appear to value sports activities as a way to affirm their competence; however, these activities often do become very competitive.

Competition. Very early in our lives we begin to compare ourselves to others and to compete with them. We also learn to value cooperation, and we will often cooperate with one group of peers in competition with another. We appear to value how we compare with others in both negative and positive ways.

Achievement. The need to achieve has been studied extensively. "Achievement motivation—the tendency to display initiative and persistence when faced with challenging tasks" (Berk, 1989, p. 472) is highly valued in all human societies and is encouraged at an early age. Achievement is encouraged in American schools through grades and other rewards.

The achievements mentioned as reasons to feel proud or happy by the children I have interviewed are successively those rewarded or approved by their parents, their peers, and then by one's self as achievement becomes internalized as a motivating value.

In the form of an accomplishment—something achieved in spite of the odds, including self-doubt and other expectations of failure—achievement is mentioned frequently as a source of pride.

Self-esteem. There is abundant evidence that we all value recognition and self-esteem. It appears as early as the preschool period. We develop feelings about various aspects of ourselves. It seems clear that we make a number of self-evaluations, that is, we develop feelings about our intelligence and academic competence, about our acceptance by our parents and peers, and about our physical abilities and appearance. Typically, we do not develop global feelings about ourselves until we acquire an integrated conception of ourselves and this does not occur prior to middle childhood; for many children, it occurs much later.

There are gender differences in self-esteem; males have more positive feelings about their physical abilities and females have more positive feelings about their reading abilities. These differences "parallel clear behavioral differences between the sexes. Boys generally out-perform girls in athletic power and skill during middle childhood whereas girls do better in school, particularly in the verbal areas" (Berk, 1989, p. 472).

There does appear to be a universal need for self-esteem because we all value recognition and approval from our peers.

Identity. The need for a coherent conception of self, identity has been described as a series of goals, values, and beliefs that become integrated into an organized, consistent self-system that is worthy of giving direction and meaning to one's life (Berk, 1989, p. 476).

This need is typically evident in adolescence; it is during this period that young people come under pressure to achieve a mature identity. But there is evidence that identity is also an issue for some children as early as age 10. For example, a 10-year-old boy said he was proud because of who his father was. Other children at this same age, both male and female, will describe what they have done or achieved as reasons to feel proud. Clearly, even at this age, they are constructing some conception of who they are: "Self development culminates during the adolescent years with the formation of an identity, a coherent, integrated conception of self consisting of self-chosen goals and values" (Berk, 1989, p. 480).

Mutuality. There comes a time for many of us when we want and value a relationship with at least one other person, possibly more, that involves mutually shared interests, beliefs, and values, and a mutual affection. Females seem to value mutuality earlier and more consistently than males do, but it is clearly valued by both genders and the gender of the other person is not a primary consideration.

At all age levels, but particularly in old age, we simply want someone with whom to share our lives. That sharing relationship is enhanced when both parties in the relationship value mutuality. I believe this need-value is highly related to our need for connections and relationships and may simply be the mature form of this need.

Autonomy. We appear to need a sense of autonomy, but males more so than females. In our culture, males are literally forced to value a sense of autonomy—a sense that they are not beholden to or dependent upon anyone else. This value appears to be linked to our conception of the individual in the Western culture. There certainly are pressures in our culture for males to be independent, self-sufficient, self-determined, self-motivated, and autonomous. The need appears to be over-determined in many American males. For many of them, it appears to conflict with mutuality as an interpersonal need.

Integrity. This need is also culturally and socially sanctioned, but it has a psychological basis as well. We seem to have what can only be described as an inborn need to be the same from one moment to the next, and to have continuity and a constancy of intention and purpose that contributes to an overall sense of integrity. Our culture requires us to be what we say we are, to do what we say we are going to do, and to keep our contracts both with ourselves and with others.

A faith to live by. This need appears to be quite universal, suggesting that it meets some strongly felt need for most people. Some people value their religion and their relationship to a god or to the universe with considerable passion. For most of us, it is a moving force in our lives. We simply cannot ignore it as a value that informs our feelings.

You will notice that I have not included our need to reproduce in this list. There is abundant evidence that we have this need; however, it is a biological need and so basic that it simply does not fit anywhere in this list of what are essentially psychological needs. It is a need that can make us uncomfortable when it is not met and very comfortable when it is met. It is also probably linked to our need for play, identity, mutuality, and spirituality. For many people, having children provides them with a sense of immortality which is, perhaps, a place where psychology and spirituality come together.

So, our needs lead to the construction of a system of values which is reflected in our feelings, and our values also appear to influence our actions—the actions that turn feelings into emotions that mediate our social interactions. As Weiner and his colleagues (1977) remind us, many psychologists regard the study of consciousness and of our needs and feelings as "antiscience ... [and that] there is a need for new scientific procedures, such as, 'experiential X rays,' that allow more direct access to the study of consciousness and feeling. To be effective and to fulfill its own potential, the humanistic approach must be guided by scientific principles" (p. 446).

I certainly agree, and I believe that in the Emotional Development Interview (EDI), which is described in Chapter 5, I have found a procedure that does provide direct access to people's consciousness with respect to their feelings and emotions.

─── 3 ───

The Psychology of Anger, Shame, Guilt, Sadness, Pride, and Happiness

The popular belief that a child's emotions do not change with growth requires the improbable assumption that maturational changes in the brain that produce new cognitive evaluations and special feeling tones have no influence on the older person's emotional experiences. (Kagan, 1984, p. 172)

Emotions are not dumb forces beyond our control but judgments we make. As such, they have conceptual and intelligent form and a *logic* that characterizes them, if only we will look for it. . . . Their "logic" is never the cold and bloodless calculations that usually deserve that title, but they have a logic all the same, a logic of living. (Solomon, 1983, pp. 251–252)

As we have seen, our feelings and emotions provide an element of form or structure to our needs and values. Each of our feelings and emotions, in turn, acquires a logic that is meaningful within the context of our social relationships and our culture. What follows is the product of a selected review of the literature on six feelings and emotions (anger, shame, guilt, sadness, pride, and happiness), my own personal clinical experience with them, and data collected through the use of several versions of the EDI.

ANGER

Tavris (1989) calls anger the misunderstood emotion because, "anger, like love, has such a potent capacity for good and evil" (p. 25). Although many people seem to believe that anger is simply and always a negative and destructive emotion that should be banished from the world, I agree with Tavris—anger can be a productive pattern of behavior. As Tavris (1989) suggests, it can be "a moral emotion" (p. 25). It often involves an effort to combat injustice or to change an unfair situation.

However, there is a curious problem with the name we have for this feeling and emotion. It appears to be misnamed. The feeling that appears to be typical of all forms of anger is that of feeling threatened, but the action upon this feeling varies considerably in the data that I have. Some people withdraw while others attack or retaliate and some people talk while others become quiet. In conventional practice it is as if we have named anger with just one way of acting upon the feeling of being threatened in mind—active retaliation, either verbal or physical.

Anger then, is a much more complex personal-social construction and each of the different forms of anger involves a somewhat different feeling and an action that is logically linked to that feeling. To study anger as a personal-social cognitive construction, males and females at ages 7 through 10, 12 through 15, and 14 through 25 were interviewed. The subjects' responses revealed the objects of their anger constructions and the actions they considered appropriate or necessary when feeling angry. And although not asked to do so, some subjects explained why they believed these actions were necessary.

Most of the anger described by males ages 7 through 10 could be considered frustration-anger or intimidation-anger. They felt angry (frustrated) because they could not do something they were trying to do or wanted to do. Their actions upon this feeling included acting out, leaving the scene, and verbalizing their frustration and asking for help. It is as if they were saying, "Why can't I do this?" or "This shouldn't be this hard."

They also felt angry (threatened) because somebody was being physically intimidating, either an adult or a peer; that is, they were being "hit," "punched," or "pushed." Feeling angry because they were being hit, punched, or pushed was the most frequently mentioned reason these males were angry. They appeared to live in a very intimidating world. As might be expected, they responded differently when intimidated by an adult rather than a peer—they responded passively to adults but rather actively to peers. The logic for the latter is to "get even."

Very prominent in the actions described by some of the 8-year-old males and many of the 9- and 10-year-old males was "telling an adult" when they had been hit, punched, or pushed. Apparently in their subculture (the school and family) there is a rule against fighting (hitting, punching, and pushing); they have accepted and internalized the rule and consider it unfair when others have not, so they report infractions. Interestingly enough, very few females in this age group suggested this as an action when they had been hit, punched, or pushed, something they described much less often than the males did. It is as if the rule is just for males and both the males and females know it.

For the males, the logic of their action seemed to be, "You shouldn't be doing that. That's not fair. We aren't supposed to do that. I'm going to tell on you." For males who prefer nonviolence and identify with the rule-makers, this action makes good sense even though some of their peers and perhaps a few adults regard this as tattletale behavior.

In the responses of the males ages 12 through 15, physical intimidation was still mentioned with some frequency but punching and pushing were more prominent than hitting and there was no mention of being physically intimidated by adults. Conflicts with peers were the most frequently mentioned reasons to be angry. These conflicts involved being lied to or called names and threats to relationships, mostly with the opposite sex. Cheating in competition was mentioned as a cause of anger, as was performing poorly and losing. But conflicts and fusses with peers that included name-calling were the dominant reasons these males felt angry. Conflicts with parents were mentioned infrequently by this group as a reason to feel angry.

The actions mentioned by these males suggested that they were, in effect, saying, "You can't get away with that. It's not something I would do. It's not true. It's against the rules and it's not fair either. We can't be friends if you do that." As one male put it, "You shouldn't do that because you wouldn't like it if I did that to you."

For the younger females, being disappointed because they did not get what they wanted or could not go and do things, and conflicts with siblings and peers, were primary objects of anger. This is in contrast to the males' concern about being physically intimidated. Their peers or siblings take, break, or lose things that belong to them; somebody teases or calls them names; or somebody is hitting or punching them (although this latter reason was mentioned five times less frequently than by males). They were also concerned about being controlled by their mothers, but they mentioned talking back to their mothers while this did not appear to be an option for males.

Younger females mentioned acting out, sometimes wildly, even more frequently than males did, but this appears short-lived and they become very verbal in their reactions to frustration, intimidation, and their mothers' efforts to control them. By 9 and 10, however, they become concerned about fighting with and losing friends, and especially about being teased, called names, and being lied about. For these females, threats to relationships were frequently mentioned as a reason for feeling angry.

For females ages 12 through 15, "rumors," "things said against them," and their reputations were the dominant reasons for feeling angry. They were also concerned about being in conflict with their peers, siblings, and parents, and they became "mad" when others did "things to them that they did not like."

Females appeared to respond to these threats by getting in a fight, which might involve a push but little more. Thus, to them a fight was more of a fuss and the exchange was more verbal than physical. Most important of all, I believe, is the fact that they feel free to "talk back" to their mothers when in conflict with them. This is quite evident in the data.

There is evidence of another gender difference that may be of some significance. Females more frequently expressed disappointment with their parents whereas males appeared to express a defensive contempt or disgust with their parents' efforts to control them. The logic that provides the structure for these anger constructions is not at all clear to me because we did not ask about it. It is made more complex by a major development that is quite evident in the data obtained from males and females ages 14 through 25: Whereas young children described feeling angry when confronted by events that were frustrating or threatening to them, at about 11 or 12 they began to characterize these events (usually another person's actions) with value-laden words that suggested irritation, annoyance, disgust, contempt, envy, jealousy, and so forth, rather than just frustration or anger as such. And more and more, the action linked to the feeling was a calibrated one; the action was psychologically linked to the degree of threat in the object of the feeling.

Males ages 14 through 25 reported feeling angry for the following reasons:

1. Parent/authority figure controlling, irritating, annoying, disgusting (25%)
2. Situation is irritating, disgusting (23%)
3. Sibling is irritating, annoying, disgusting (19%)
4. Girlfriend lied to, cheated on, let down (11%)
5. Had accident, loss, or breakdown with car or boat (9%)
6. Made mistake, was doing (did) poorly (8%)

Females ages 14 through 25 reported feeling angry for the following reasons:

1. Parent(s) disappointing, frustrating, controlling (23%)
2. Friend (same sex) annoying, irritating, disappointing, frustrating (20%)
3. Treated unfairly, taken advantage of by peers, co-workers, authority figures (20%)
4. Sibling annoying, irritating, disappointing (15%)
5. Boyfriend lied to, cheated on, let down (12%)

It was somewhat surprising to see that the actions of the subjects' parents were so frequently a reason for anger. It suggests that the struggle for autonomy, which I thought occurred earlier, is a major issue for young people at this age.

The other thing I find impressive in this data is the emphasis on relationships in the anger constructions for the females. Almost all of their constructions involve relationships; this is in contrast to the males' concerns about situations, possessions, boats, cars, and performance. Males also find the behavior of their siblings annoying, irritating, and disgusting, and they anger when they are lied to, cheated on, or let down by their girlfriends. On the other hand, females are far more often angry in their relationships with their same-sex peers and when they believe they are being treated unfairly or being taken advantage of by their peers, co-workers, or authority figures (their male teachers, for example).

This concern for relationships is very striking; it is beautifully expressed in one female's description of her recent experience feeling angry:

I was angry because my work partner decided two days before a long weekend that she needed to take off to go away with her boyfriend. I told her if she needed to go then she should. I held in my angry feelings at her to resolve them by myself. I have a terrific working relationship with her and I didn't want to jeopardize it.

But, as mentioned earlier, a development that is very evident in the anger constructions of these subjects is the appearance of value-laden words in their descriptions of both other people's actions and their own actions as well. Much of their anger has the logic of irritation, annoyance, contempt, resentment, envy, and jealousy. In Chapter 1, I described how jealousy becomes differentiated from envy and anger. This is what appears to occur with irritation, annoyance, contempt, and so forth; their construction depends upon the acquisition of new conceptions of one's relationships. Almost all of the actions these young adults take on these feelings are verbal in nature except that they also report turning away in disgust and contempt, and females report "cutting off"— just not talking to the person whose actions they find offensive. They also describe talking it out and making up as ways of managing these threatening situations.

My data, limited as it is by the fact that we asked too few questions and had too small a sample, clearly support the notion that the objects of anger change with maturation and social experience; that there are gender similarities and differences; and that anger constructions become highly differentiated, more abstract in nature, and much more flexible and adaptive with development.

Rage

It is rage that probably gave anger its bad name. We did not ask about rage but I have observed it and I have had personal and professional experience with it.

Almost all infants and young children rage at one time or another. They do so when some need is frustrated and their initial effort to deal with the frustrating event is ineffective. In infancy and early childhood, rage is an effort, typically a desperate one, to deal with events that are recognized or known intuitively to be very threatening. More and more energy is mobilized and it overwhelms the system, so to speak, and the child goes out of control. Help from outside the system is often needed to calm the child and bring its energy utilization back into healthy limits. Cognitive and conceptual factors have only a limited role in rage at this stage of development.

Although rage as a distinctive form of anger has received little attention and is therefore poorly understood, it seems clear that adult rage has a conceptual (cognitive) component. When I encounter rage in my professional practice and talk with clients about it, I am always a little surprised at how highly justified it is. They feel that they have a "damn good reason to be mad!" and the reason usually turns out to be an injustice they believe they are being subjected to. (Sometimes, of course, the belief is realistic.) "How can they (you) do that to me?" they will ask. There is often an accompanying sense of desperation, but the feeling that their rage is justified is often so strong that they are not conscious of their rage. They are startled when it is called to their attention.

Unfortunately, rage is often followed by violent, destructive behavior, behavior that is also so well justified that it seems "natural" to the person involved. Can rage be tamed? Can it be reconstructed into something prosocial and positive? The answer to both questions is yes. It can become a passionate devotion to the elimination of injustice and therefore the very essence of morality. To do so, the feeling of hopelessness and of desperation must be addressed and changed.

SHAME AND GUILT

The logic of shame and guilt is quite similar, but as people describe these two feelings there are often important differences that are ignored. According to theorists (Izard, 1977; Kaufman, 1992; Tomkins, 1987; Harper & Hoopes, 1990), the logic of shame involves the belief that one is inferior or flawed in some significant way, while the logic of guilt involves the belief that one has done something "wrong" or "bad." Both shame and guilt then, are believed to be moral feelings and emotions.

My own research on these two feelings and emotions reveals that many young children do not have the word "guilt" in their vocabulary. If you ask them if they ever feel guilty they look puzzled, but if you ask them if they ever feel ashamed they respond immediately. However, when you ask them why they felt ashamed, many of them give reasons that have the logic of either shame or guilt. Apparently, many parents teach their children to feel ashamed and/or guilty by shaming them.

Shame

It seems clear that guilt is adaptive and so is shame, if the feeling is briefly held, so to speak. However, shame can be a very destructive feeling and emotion because it is often constructed early and involves, as it does, the belief that one is flawed or inferior in some significant way, which then influences all of one's actions and relationships.

These two feelings and emotions are poorly differentiated cognitive constructions for many children up to about age 8. Many children do not differentiate among anger, shame, guilt, and sadness; this was especially true for the females that were interviewed. At least thirty-five percent of the females did not differentiate between shame and anger; they equated shame with frustration and suggested some very destructive actions, that is, hitting, breaking, ripping, and "writing all over the wall" (!) as ways of dealing with frustrating events and situations.

By age 8, many children's constructions for these two feelings have a different logic. They felt guilty about doing the wrong thing or something that they regarded as bad, or that hurt others. Males felt ashamed when others didn't like them or didn't want to play with them, but females felt ashamed because they had something wrong with them.

At age 9, neither males nor females gave reasons for feeling ashamed that included the logic of shame. We asked them about shame and they gave us reasons that reflected the logic of guilt.

At age 10, males were ashamed because of their appearance or because others were critical of them, and females were ashamed for this latter reason (more often than males) and because of their appearance (their clothes were ripped, split, or dirty).

Between ages 12 and 15, males felt ashamed for several reasons; others were critical of them, they performed poorly compared to others, or their parents didn't approve of something they had done. Females felt ashamed for performing poorly compared to others and when their secrets were revealed.

At age 15, both males and females had acquired the concept of being embarrassed, and they were embarrassed because of their appearance or because they had done something that others considered "dumb" or "weird."

Beginning at age 12 then, the reasons one feels ashamed or embarrassed begin to resemble the reasons one also feels guilty—appearances or actions which can be changed or covered up. It appears that the reasons for feeling ashamed, which were dominant at an earlier age (not being liked, being criticized, and having something wrong with one's self), are now subsumed under being embarrassed, and that these more painful feelings about one's self are being denied.

Moreover, the logic of shame has a curious transformation. Implicit in young children's reasons for feeling ashamed is the belief that they are different or inferior in some significant way and that they cannot do anything about it so they withdraw, go off by themselves, or play with their own things.

Then at age 9, no reasons for shame are given; there is only the logic of guilt.

At age 10, shame reappears but it has undergone a transformation. The reasons one feels ashamed are that others are critical of one's actions and/or appearance. How one feels about one's self is not important; rather, how one appears to others is what counts and this contributes to the acquisition of the concept of embarrassment. The logic of shame has been replaced by the logic of embarrassment.

The abstract generalization that captures the essence of shame is that we feel ashamed when we believe that we are flawed in some significant way and are therefore unworthy or insignificant. Typically, at all levels, feeling ashamed is acted upon by an effort to hide or cover up, or to avoid embarrassment. A mature shame leads us to avoid embarrassment and disgrace—which makes us more fully human. Knowing shame, we are more humane in our treatment of others.

Guilt

My data suggest that the logic of guilt eventually becomes differentiated from the logic of shame. Young children feel guilty because they believe they have done something "wrong" or "bad." They try to undo what they have done and/or they turn to an adult for help.

In middle childhood, they feel guilty because they have done something they "shouldn't" do, and near the end of middle childhood something they *knew* they "shouldn't" do. They either say they are sorry or they try to deny it or to hide the fact that they did it.

By preadolescence, children feel guilty because they have lied, cheated, or stolen something and they expect to be punished; in some cases, they punish themselves. It is as if they have internalized a logic that declares: "Lying, cheating, and/or stealing are wrong and bad, and something everybody knows you shouldn't do, so you have to be punished if you do it." They expect to be punished; they may reject or punish those who lie, cheat, and/or steal, and they may punish themselves if no one else does.

Many adolescents idealize being honest, sensitive to others, or, in some idealized way, "good," and trying to live up to these ideals is simply not enough. They are unforgiving and very hard on themselves, and this can make adolescence a very painful period in their lives.

Mature adults are more inclined to consider the circumstances surrounding their transgressions. They apologize more readily, make restitution if possible, and/or forgive themselves and others for their transgressions.

Denial appears to be the critical variable at all levels of development in the difference between productive (healthy) and unproductive (unhealthy) guilt.

In mature guilt, individuals recognize and take responsibility for their "wrong" or "bad" behavior and they accept the consequences that follow from these actions. Also, mature adults know what acts will make them feel guilty and they avoid them.

In immature guilt, individuals may recognize that their behavior was "wrong" or "bad" but they resist all responsibility for these actions. They may try to cover up their transgressions and may even try to get others to help them do so.

Some individuals may even resist accepting the fact that they did something that would cause most people to feel guilty. Shame seems to be involved here. It is as if they are saying to themselves, "I just can't stand being wrong (or bad) again." When people resist guilt, look for shame—it is usually there.

There are some recently published materials on the recognition and treatment of guilt and shame, for example, R. Potter-Efron and P. Potter-Efron (1989), Borysenko (1990), Harper and Hoopes (1990), and Middelton-Moz (1990). These materials offer excellent suggestions for treating unhealthy shame and guilt that are consistent with the perspective I am presenting here.

SADNESS

As with anger, sadness is a whole family of feelings and emotions, including sorrow, melancholy, grief, dejection, discouragement, and depression. However, sadness is a more complex feeling than anger because some forms of sadness are more a mood than a feeling—a mood that colors a person's perception of events and actions.

The logic of sadness is quite complex. We are sad when we are ill or injured, or when someone we know is ill or injured. We are sorry and we grieve if that person dies. We are sad when we are alone, without friends, or when we lose a friend.

We are also frustrated, upset, discouraged, or even depressed when we don't have or can't get something we need or want, and when we can't go and do something that we want to do. When we are punished, we are also depressed if we regard our situation as hopeless and we feel helpless.

The feeling (belief) that the situation we are confronting is hopeless and that we are helpless appears to be a common element across all forms of sadness. Thus, loss does not seem to be the sole element in all sadness, as suggested by Solomon (1983); the logic of sadness is more complicated than that. The data I have from children ages 7 through 15 certainly support this conclusion.

When asked about sadness, 7-year-old children described three reasons for feeling sad. In the order of the frequency in which they were mentioned, these were: (a) discouragement in the form of not having or getting what they want, or not being able to go somewhere or to do something that interests them; (b) sadness at being lost, alone, or without friends; and (c) sorrow when someone is ill or injured. Neither males nor females mentioned death.

As reactions for (a), the children either withdrew and cried, often going off by themselves, or they distracted themselves by doing something else. For (b), they tried to find another friend, asked an adult for help, or just played by themselves in resignation. And for (c), they put a bandage on the injury, sought adult help, or cried.

At age 8, males mentioned being discouraged because they "don't have," "can't get," "can't go," or "can't do." They also gave " being yelled at" or "being punished" as reasons to be sad.

At ages 9 and 10, the most frequently-mentioned reasons for feeling sad in the form of sorrow and grief were illness, injury, and death. Females also mentioned having one's feelings hurt as a reason to feel sad; males did not.

Both males and females responded to feeling sad by crying, going off by themselves, or confiding in an adult. Some had learned that they should try to console a person who is ill or hurt, or who has lost someone through death. A few mentioned sending a card or flowers.

At age 9, when confronted with illness, injury, or death, males mentioned crying, taking care of the injury, seeking help, or telling another person that they are sorry. About half of the females mentioned crying and going off by themselves; the other half mentioned making an effort to deal with the injury, including getting a bandage and seeking help. Both males and females either passively accepted being punished or they got "mad."

As mentioned above, sorrow and grief were the dominant forms of sadness for 10-year-old children except that females were very concerned with being lonely and without friends. As a response, they tried to repair friendships or make new friends, or they simply accepted being alone. At this age they didn't mention crying.

As a response to illness, injury, and death, males mentioned prayer for the first time, along with seeking help and trying to console others by sending a card or just going to visit. When feeling sorrow or grief, both males and females seemed sensitive to the idea of actively consoling the other person or seeking the presence of another person.

Two new situations were mentioned by males as reasons to be sad: (a) doing something they regret, and (b) someone else having something they want, as in envy. Interestingly enough, females also mentioned "doing something wrong" as a reason to feel sad. Both males and females recognized the need to say they were sorry when they regretted some action, and they were typically moved to try harder when feeling envious. For some children at this age then, sadness and guilt have a logic similar to sadness and envy.

Between ages 8 and 10, however, the dominant logic of sadness was sorrow and grief in situations where relatively little can be done except adapt, for example, to the irreversibility of an illness, injury, or death. Females mentioned having one's feelings hurt while males mentioned losing a valued object as other reasons to be sad. While initially "upset," males mentioned actively trying to repair or change these situations.

What is puzzling was the appearance of so many situations that were also mentioned in the logic of anger. This occurred throughout the age range of 7 through 10. Does this occur because children acquire what is essentially a passive resignation, colored by feelings of hopelessness and helplessness, into which they assimilate these interpersonal situations of being frustrated, being punished, and for the females, having one's feelings hurt? I also wonder if the basic logic of some forms of depression is not constructed in this way at this stage of development.

What is most interesting is that some of these children also reported feeling upset (or temporarily sad?) in many situations where they might have said they were angry. In these situations, many went on to indicate that following this upset they were then angry and did something assertive.

What is also interesting is that sadness or depression in the form of being upset, when followed by some assertive, determined action, is probably a very productive sadness or depression; it is probably more productive than impulsive anger would be. Gut

(1989) has suggested that depression can be productive or unproductive in just this way. What must be involved here is the habit of evaluating situations as hopeless, and believing that one is therefore helpless, that is acquired when one is forced to adapt to circumstances beyond one's control (illness, hurt, injury, or death).

Then, between ages 10 and 12, a change in the logic of sadness that reflects these considerations appears to take place; sorrow and grief no longer dominate.

For children ages 12 through 15, difficulties with friends and struggles with parents for autonomy were the dominant reasons to be sad in the form of being discouraged or depressed. Both of these situations were also very evident in the logic of anger.

When having difficulty with friends, both males and females reported turning away and withdrawing, or making an active effort to surmount the difficulty by making up or finding another friend. They provided many examples of productive sadness or depression in which "upset" was followed by an assertive effort.

They also frequently described themselves as upset in their struggles with their parents (remember, this is in response to being asked about feeling sad). Real fusses were described in which they either passively accepted their parents' wishes, assertively demanded to be heard, or became angry and sometimes left the scene.

At this age, there is little difference in the logic of sadness for males and females except that females appear to be less inclined to get angry. Females also appear to do more to protect and repair relationships.

Sadness then, begins to be a habitual way of relating to events and situations, and it can be productive or unproductive.

By adulthood, sadness in the form of discouragement about one's failures in a competition or a creative endeavor, and the loss or prospective loss of a relationship (a friendship) has a distinctive logic and ethic. In adulthood, failure and loss, or the prospect of failure and loss, are critical in the logic of sadness. Many adults see sorrow or grief at the loss of a significant other through death as different than sadness. They appear to regard sorrow and grief as different feelings and emotions.

Failure in a competition or a creative endeavor and difficulties with relationships are also situations in which many people anger. What seems to be critical in determining whether one is angry or sad is how one reflects upon the situation. Some people view failure and loss as challenges; others seem to develop a habit of responding to failure and loss with resignation and withdrawal, and they develop a sense of helplessness.

However, Gut (1989) suggests that sadness, even as depression, can serve a positive function. As a temporary withdrawal from our usual activities, it can be a time of sober self-evaluation that can provide the basis for a new, more responsible and autonomous selfhood. The sadness or mild depression that follows the loss of a contest, a competition, or some other effort to achieve a particular goal can also be a time of constructive self-evaluation, a time when new goals are set, and a time when alternative strategies are studied and planned.

In the logic and ethic of sadness and depression, as it appears in my clinical experience and in my interview data, some people seem to develop a habit of responding to many situations with resignation, withdrawal, and a sense of helplessness. This way of reacting is probably more of a personality variable or just a habit than it is a stage of development. What is critical, however, is that the habit of negatively evaluating situations as hopeless and oneself as helpless (both feelings that are synonymous with feeling sad) is, in itself, something that needs to be dealt with.

Seen this way, sadness appears to have a different logic and ethic than do anger and guilt. In anger and guilt, it is usually important to try to change the situation that makes one feel angry or guilty. In sadness (and depression) it is probably more important to focus one's efforts on trying to change the negative cognitive evaluations that lead to withdrawal, resignation, and helplessness. This is the focus of the cognitive theory of depression advanced by Beck (1976).

In adulthood then, sadness (depression) is essentially a way of relating to failure and loss and, in its transitional form, it can serve a productive function. A mature sadness can be the pause that provides time for us to reorganize and reconstitute ourselves.

PRIDE AND HAPPINESS

Whereas the negative emotions are emotions we construct to deal with situations that we would change if we could, pride and happiness are emotions we construct to enjoy and prolong, if possible. Strangely enough, however, although most people indicate that when proud they feel more generous toward others, a number of people have difficulty letting themselves feel proud. They appear to accept the biblical injunction against pride as if pride always involves arrogance and contempt for others. From the data I have collected from children ages 7 through 15, this is definitely not the case. Almost all of them reported being more kind and generous toward others when they felt proud.

Happiness is similar to pride in many ways in that, beginning in middle childhood, it involves achievement that enables one to feel good about one's self and one's well-being. Children described being happy when they have been successful or have won in a competition with others, but proud when they have done so against the odds, their own self-doubt, or the predictions of others that they would fail. Thus, the logic of happiness involves achievement and the logic of pride involves a sense of accomplishment.

Let us look briefly at the logic of these two positive emotions.

Pride

Pride involves making a positive evaluation of one's self. In many ways, pride can be seen as constituting an antidote to shame. One feels worthy, valued, and accomplished as opposed to feeling unworthy, devalued, and a failure. Pride is also an antidote to sadness and depression.

In the course of development, transformations in the logic of pride are limited, for the most part, to changes in the source of the positive evaluation of one's self. At all age levels, the reasons for feeling proud are quite similar and involve essentially three things: (a) the realization that one has accomplished something, (b) the recognition that one has done something commendable, and (c) the realization that one is fortunate.

Until about age 8, children get their sense of accomplishment from their parents and other authority figures. They enjoy getting something right, for example, making an A or winning a race, because their parents praise them for doing so. They feel good about their behavior and their acts of cooperation and sharing because adults regard this as commendable behavior and tell them so in many ways.

By ages 9 and 10, the locus of these positive value judgments is shifted to the peer group. Increasingly, the peer group value system is the source of children's evaluation of their achievements and their social behavior. As I have noted elsewhere (Dupont, 1989), the need for the peer group can lead to a rigidly conformist approach to the evaluation of the actions of self and others. Children are often cruel to one another because they take the rules and standards of the group very seriously, and they have not yet achieved a role-taking perspective.

In the middle school and early high school years, children acquire the ability to put themselves in the other person's shoes and they adopt the golden rule of doing to others as they would have others do to them; thus, they value reciprocity.

Sometime during the high school years, most young people internalize the peer group's tried and tested values. This internalized value system, which they are continually refining, becomes the reference for their evaluation of their behavior and the source of their pride, shame, or guilt.

In adulthood, mutuality, autonomy, and integrity can be idealized and valued, and their realization can be a source of pride, self-esteem, and a sense of well-being. A mature feeling of pride involves the conception that one has accomplished something of value or that one possesses something of unique or special value, and it is often accompanied by more positive feelings and actions toward others.

Happiness

Like feeling proud, feeling happy is a positive feeling state that has been thought about and written about throughout the long history of civilization. Some philosophers have suggested that happiness should not be pursued directly; rather, we should lose ourselves in pursuit of some higher purpose and happiness will just come to us. Others have equated happiness with wealth and success, making it an end product of a deliberate effort. As such, happiness can be fleeting because wealth and success can be elusive.

More recently, Csikszentmihalyi (1990) has reviewed the conclusions he has reached about the nature of happiness after years of studying the phenomenon worldwide. In the course of his studies, Csikszentmihalyi (1990) developed "a theory of optimal experience based on the concept of *flow*—the state in which people are so involved in an activity that nothing else seems to matter; the experience itself is so enjoyable that people will do it even at great cost, for the sheer sake of doing it" (p. 4).

Defined in this way, happiness is something we can deliberately create for ourselves by controlling our conscious experience. Interestingly enough, seen in this light, it is very similar to the effective performance state deliberately created by many of the world's best athletes. They focus on and imagine a positive performance, and then use relaxation techniques to stay relaxed but alert during a competition. This deliberate manipulation of the content of their consciousness produces a feeling of being "in the zone" that is similar to the feeling of flow.

In everyday experience, this is similar to the feeling that one is doing well and all is going well. This emphasis on the quality of an ongoing experience as the critical element of happiness is certainly different than the child's notion that happiness is getting what you want.

My data suggest that the following transformations occur in the logic of happiness.

In early childhood, happiness is having or getting what you want; for example, it is your birthday or Christmas and you get everything you want. Happiness is also going where you want to go or doing what you want to do.

In middle childhood, achievement and having friends to do things with are an important source of happiness. Getting something valued is still an essential ingredient of happiness, but it is overshadowed by achievement and having friends. And some children relate happiness to joking around, laughing, and having fun.

In preadolescence, achievement and having or getting something valued are the most frequently mentioned reasons to be happy. In contrast to childhood, where presents that provide immediate gratification are valued, in preadolescence bicycles and other items with utilitarian value are preferred.

Early in adolescence, achievement and involvement with the opposite sex begin to be critical elements for happiness. There is also a change in how achievement is defined. When first mentioned in middle childhood, achievement is that performance which is praised by adults. Then achievement that compares favorably with others' achievements becomes valued; there is a comparative-competitive theme here. Then there is a shift to how one's performance compares with one's potential best—not "Was I better than you?" but "Was I doing well for me?"

The transformations in the value system noted earlier are noted again in the logic of happiness. The achievements one is happy about are those praised by adults, then those recognized by peers, and then those evaluated against an internalized value system that often includes a comparison with one's idealized best.

The logic of happiness for many adults includes those two elements that also appear in the logic of adolescent happiness: (a) having a satisfying involvement with another person, and (b) doing something well that is valued. "I'm doing well and things are going well" is the way this is often described. The latter is close to flow, but for many adults having a relationship that involves mutual regard is also important. Females, however, typically rank this higher in importance than do males.

Is there a relationship between feeling proud and feeling happy? I can believe that there is. People without pride (or self-esteem) probably find it hard to believe that they are doing well and that things are going well. This is an empirical question, of course, and one that we should study.

SOME RELATIONSHIPS BETWEEN FEELINGS

Beginning as early as age 9 or 10, as children begin to achieve an abstract, self-reflective consciousness, they also begin to evaluate their own feelings and to have feelings about their feelings. Even before this, they may construct a feeling as a defense against another feeling. For example, some people become angry when confronted with experiences that may be embarrassing. And in my experience, quite often there are people who feel guilty or ashamed of being angry, people who feel guilty because they have allowed themselves to feel proud, and people who are disgusted with themselves or feel contempt for themselves because they have failed.

I have also observed people who cannot allow themselves to feel guilty because it verifies their shame—their sense of being inferior or flawed in some way. This ability to be conscious of and to reflect upon one's feelings is a developmental achievement, but when kept to oneself some feelings, shame in particular, can be very painful. I suspect that this is what is often involved in adolescent depression and adult depression as well.

Also, what may appear to be simply discouragement, shame, or depression may also have an element of anger toward self and others. I believe these mixed feelings are a result of having needs and values that are not cognized and clarified, and that are therefore conflicting. Becoming clear about their values and feelings, and then making good choices in how they want to express their feelings and how they want to realize their values in their relationships must be one of the major challenges of adolescence.

All of these observations about these relationships between feelings are personal impressions that I would like to see verified.

COMMENTS

These data support the notion that our feelings and emotions change as a function of our maturation and social experience, and that there are gender differences in our feelings and emotions, perhaps because males and females have different needs and values. There also appear to be transformations in the logic of our respective feelings and emotions, but our present understanding is based on our subjects having voluntarily given us reasons for their actions and on inferences drawn from their answers to our two questions. Using the longer interview with six questions for the negative feelings and five questions for the positive feelings provides a much more comprehensive and detailed picture of how our needs and values inform our feelings and emotions.

Each feeling reviewed in this chapter is linked to a concern about the well-being or identity of an agent-self. All of these feelings concern the self's evaluation of ongoing events and situations that contribute to the construction of the various emotions that mediate all of our self-world interactions. Each feeling and emotion has a different logic but each one serves the self. The logic of our respective feelings and emotions becomes an element in our consciousness, which is increasingly conceptually abstract.

—— **4** ——

Development, Social Experience, and Consciousness

Life is essentially autoregulation. (Piaget, 1971, p. 26)

Before anything becomes a mental function proper, located "within" an individual, it must first exist externally, as an exchange between two people. (Shotter, 1975, p. 101)

It is by the character of his consciousness that he [man] distinguishes himself from all else that there is. (Shotter, 1975, pp. 40–41)

DEVELOPMENT

Piaget and Inhelder (1969) identified two processes (assimilation and accommodation) that are involved in cognitive development and, therefore, in emotional development as well. Assimilation is perhaps the most basic of these processes, as illustrated in this conversation Piaget had with Bringuier (1980):

Bringuier: Would you explain what assimilation is and what accommodation is?

Piaget: Well, assimilation is just the proof that structures exist. It's the fact that a stimulus from the external world, any excitant, can act on or modify behavior only to the degree that it is integrated with prior structures. Assimilation is chiefly a biological concept. By digesting food, the organism assimilates the environment; this means that the environment is subordinated to the internal structure and not the reverse.

Bringuier: If I eat a cabbage, I don't become a cabbage—is that it?

Piaget: Yes. A rabbit that eats a cabbage doesn't become a cabbage; it's the cabbage that becomes rabbit—that's assimilation. It's the same thing at the psychological level. Whatever the stimulus is, it is integrated with internal structures. (p. 42)

Cognitive development is an internal process of construction, and since feelings and emotions are cognitive constructions, emotional development is also a process of construction. As products of constructions, our feelings and emotions are transformed in the course of development.

But, and this is a very important but, we are never without constructions. We start with very primitive, wired-in constructions that become, through the processes of assimilation and accommodation, an elaborate system of feelings and emotions that mediates all of our interactions with our world.

Of considerable importance then, is this: When confronted with a new event, situation, or object, we try to assimilate it to constructions we already have. For example, I have never met you before so, at first, I will feel about you the way I do toward that person you most remind me of. This is simply inevitable and it is one of our basic characteristics. We typically do this without realizing that we are doing it. We assimilate new events, situations, and objects to the feelings we already have. Then we change our feelings about them to accommodate ourselves to their unique characteristics.

This same thing happens with our actions upon our feelings. Initially, we act upon a feeling about a particular event, situation, or object the way we usually act upon this feeling. We change our actions when we develop a different understanding of the event, situation, or object.

But where our feelings and emotions are concerned, this understanding is not the same cold, objective understanding (or intelligence) that we acquire for the world of physical objects, but it is a subjective understanding of both our world of personal objects and of a social world, because there are other persons like ourselves in that world.

As Gallagher and Reid (1981) remind us, the development of our understanding of that personal-social world proceeds through the processes of empirical abstraction and reflexive abstraction. We learn to identify and label our feelings and emotions, not as physical objects but as personal-social processes. Then, through reflexive abstraction in company with others, we construct rules and principles which give order and structure to our understanding of our feelings and emotions. This understanding (or intelligence) becomes a personal intelligence when it is filtered through our feelings and it becomes our personal consciousness.

Therefore, our consciousness always has a conceptual element because our understanding (or intelligence) is always conceptual in nature, and, as we shall see, our consciousness contributes to the construction and reconstruction of our feelings and emotions. Both our consciousness and our emotional development are products of our social experience.

SOCIAL EXPERIENCE

In the course of our lives we have a succession of social experiences that are important for our emotional development. These experiences are social in that they always involve other persons, one or more at a time. A social experience with another person is usually called a relationship, and some theorists have suggested that the relationship itself is critical for our emotional development.

Piaget and Inhelder (1969), however, suggest that it is the interaction between the persons involved in the relationship that is critical for development. As an example, they discuss the work of Spitz who had noticed that when children in charitable institutions were separated from their mothers they often became retarded or arrested in their development. When this separation was permanent, some children regressed to very infantile states. Spitz attributed the arrest, retardation, and regression to the absence of the mother. Piaget and Inhelder (1969) argue that we must consider all of the factors that may be involved in this phenomenon. They suggest that it is the "lack of stimulating interactions" that causes the retardation and regression, not simply the "maternal element" (p. 27).

A conclusion similar to this has been reached by those studying attachment. Originally the attachment itself was considered to be the critical variable in child behavior and development. Now the parent-child interaction in the attachment relationship is being studied, and these studies are producing considerable evidence that what happens in this interaction is important for the child's emotional development.

Now, you may ask, what takes place in these social experiences with other persons that is germane to emotional development? For one thing, there is discourse. As Dunn and Brown (1991) discovered in their studies of children as young as 2 interacting with their parents, this discourse involves children making comments on their own affective states and asking questions about their parents' affective states and others' affective states. From observations of my own daughter interacting with her four children, I know that some parents provide names for these affective states. They label them as feelings or emotions, thus making it easier to talk about them and to link them to ongoing events. In this discourse, children's natural tendency to construct coherent meaning in their lives is facilitated.

But before children begin this discourse, they have what are essentially action-scheme level feelings and emotions. Children do seem to acquire action schemes that work for them within their families at a very early age. "They [2-year-olds] seem to have developed a standard inventory of social-interaction patterns to use within the family" (White & Watts, 1973, p. 237). These social-interaction patterns almost certainly have an intuitive level logic about them that corresponds to the logic of our feelings and emotions after the acquisition of language and the construction of a consciousness that is conceptual in nature. They also help children maintain some kind of equilibrium in their families as they construct more flexible patterns of feeling and action that are increasingly under their conscious control. With the transformation of the logic of the various feelings and emotions, children's conscious control becomes more abstract and flexible, as was discussed in Chapter 3.

In most families, discourse is typically informal and is often conducted on the fly (so to speak), but it can become formal when parents set aside time for discussion at meals or other quality time together. Sometimes this discussion can become genuine dialogue.

Children also carry on considerable discourse with both their siblings and their peers. Without adult guidance, this discourse can become very negative and destructive as children tease and make cruel comments to one another that reflect their poor role-taking skills. This can have tragic consequences (Dupont, 1989).

Many of the children, however, talk with one another about very personal things and about their experiences with one another. This input to their thinking about themselves is the basis for their reflexive abstractions and the creation of the structure or the logic of their various feelings and emotions.

But this thinking is not simply all at the same level of abstraction. There are different levels of consciousness involved which have to do with the kinds of self-regulations children can make in their emotional behavior. Let us now examine self-regulation and consciousness.

SELF-REGULATION AND CONSCIOUSNESS

All persons have the power to regulate their actions. We are a self-regulatory system at all levels of functioning—the physiological, the behavioral, the psychological, and the psychosocial.

One of our other unique abilities, the one that distinguishes us from animals, is our consciousness. We can be conscious of ourselves and we do so at several different levels, which are related to the kind of self-regulations we can make.

At the physiological level, we are not conscious of the automatic regulations and adaptations we are capable of making. But because these auto-regulations are automatic and not under conscious control, some of them are dangerous.

This was made clear in a recent article in *The New England Journal of Medicine* in which Anand and Hickey (1992) report a study they completed on the use of anesthesia to protect newborns from pain during surgery. For some time doctors have followed the recommendations of minimizing the use of anesthetics for their infant patients.

However, in this study, which was conducted with newborns undergoing heart surgery from 1987 through 1990, it was found that survival was best for those infants who were administered deep anesthesia. All thirty babies receiving deep anesthesia survived while four of fifteen babies receiving standard light anesthesia died after surgery.

The doctors found that the babies getting light anesthesia produced high levels of stress hormones and were more prone to infections, blood clotting, and acid build-up in their muscles. It seems likely, said the researchers, that stress hormones, while useful in brief bursts when needed to cope with danger, are unhealthy when high amounts are produced for days at a time as occurred when the babies experienced pain.

Pain is a signal of danger in the infant's system that brings an automatic response (stress hormones that are produced as long as pain is experienced) but prolonged pain causes too much stress hormone to be created in the system and the result is disregulation. Because an infant's consciousness is primitive and limited, the assistance of an outside agent is required to keep its equilibrium within healthy limits. While we are persons with a psychosocial identity, we are also living systems that make many automatic physiological regulations which are essentially not under any conscious control.

We also make behavior self-regulations that are largely an adaptation to the ecological or social context in which we are living. These adaptations are so context-dominated (we are literally born into them) that little conscious self-regulation is required. And we usually have great difficulty explaining to anyone, ourselves included, just why these particular actions are necessary. They just are. According to Piaget (1976b), this is the level of self-regulation of actions without conceptualization: "[This] system of schemes [of action] . . . constitutes an elaborate know how" (p. 349). For example, I have known persons gifted in repairing things who could show me how to repair something but could not tell me how to do it.

In the sphere of interpersonal relationships, this level of self-regulation and consciousness is likely to produce reasoning like, "He hit me—I hit him." "He took mine—I took his." Or, perhaps more socially appropriate, "He hit me so I left," or "He stole one of my tools so I never let him in my workshop again." And the rationale for these actions is considered self-evident.

However, there is a third level of self-regulation and consciousness. For example, George and Jim are friends, but one day George is in a bad mood and he hits and pushes Jim. Jim fights back to show George that he just won't allow him to treat him that way. "After all," Jim reasons, "if I allow George to do that, I will lose my self-respect." I prefer to call this the psychological level of self-consciousness. Jim has a psychological reason for his actions that is logical and psychologically sound so far as it goes.

Then there is a fourth level of self-regulation and consciousness. Again, for example, George and Jim are friends. Before encountering George, Jim learns from a mutual acquaintance that George is in a foul mood. George's alcoholic parents had a fight the night before and his mother is in the hospital and his father is in jail. George had called the police for help.

Jim knows a lot of psychology for a 14-year-old because his mother is a psychologist. Jim, then, is not really surprised when George hits him and pushes him when he asks George about his parents. When George hits and pushes him some more, Jim doesn't really fight back; rather, Jim tries to fend off George's blows and pushes until he can get both of his arms around George in a bear hug at which time he says, "George, I'm sorry about your mother." George bursts into tears. Jim relaxes his bear hug, and with his arm around George's shoulder he asks, "Are you okay? Do you need a place to stay?"

In this situation, Jim is illustrating the self-reflective level of consciousness. He regulated or scripted his actions to fit his goal, which was to help his friend who was in distress. Jim took more than just his own needs into account—he was sensitive to George's needs as well. Jim could put himself into George's shoes and although Jim had never had an experience such as the one George was living, he could imagine how George felt and he had some idea of what George needed—some support from a friend (knowing, of course, that at first George might deny that he needed any help and might even reject it in an angry way).

Jim's reasons for his actions in this situation are logical and they encompass both psychological and social considerations. Jim is conscious of both his own needs and feelings and of the needs and feelings of those around him. The scripts he creates for himself take both into account, and he can reflect upon the probable consequences of his actions. His is a self-reflective consciousness.

Is this typical for a 14-year-old male? Perhaps not, but I have seen it in young people at this age. It is possible and it is certainly desirable.

These examples of different levels of self-regulation and consciousness show what I am certain is true. Higher levels of consciousness involve more comprehensive, "intentionally ordered information" (Csikszentmihalyi, 1990, p. 26). At its lowest level, there is just some registration of pain which triggers stress hormones or other auto-regulations. At the behavioral level, there is simply an awareness that something doesn't fit or that something is missing. Imagery is often involved here and we act to bring the imagery back to wholeness or symmetry. At the psychological level of self-consciousness we act to meet our psychological needs, and at the self-reflective level we act to meet the needs of others as well as our own. We can reflect upon ourselves as a part of a larger social system of other selves or persons, and we are conscious of them as persons with needs and feelings similar to our own.

Some theorists suggest that we come to be conscious of ourselves by understanding others first and then recognizing that because we are like them that what is true of them must be true of us as well. In fact, "we become ourselves through others," says Shotter (1975, p. 101).

This suggests that a human infant becomes a person in relationships with other persons and in no other way. I regard this as one of the most interesting issues in psychology today. Is our psychological growth from infancy to adulthood simply the development or unfolding of something already there, or does this growth into personhood involve taking things unto ourselves from our relationships and our culture?

SOCIAL EXPERIENCE AGAIN

As we shall see, consciousness and social experience are interrelated in some very interesting ways.

Children's social experiences change considerably in the normal course of development. Their challenge is to adapt to these changes by constructing those feelings and emotions that will create and maintain their equilibrium in the face of these changes.

Children's first relationships are heteronomous, that is, subject to external controls and impositions. In this relationship, children will develop a unilateral respect (and there is sometimes an element of fear to that respect) for their caretakers and they will construct feelings and emotions that reflect this respect.

For example, Gussie, a 9-nine-year-old female, suggested this construction for anger:

She's angry at her mother for not letting her stay up and watch her favorite program. [What will she do next?] Probably next week ask her mother "Please" and not be so mad at her mother. Maybe she got mad at her mother earlier and that's why she couldn't watch her favorite program.

Katie, a 10-year-old female, offered this construction for anger:

She asked if she could go someplace, but her mother wouldn't let her. [What will she do next?] Go up to her room and slam the door.

Rodney, an 8-year-old male, offered this construction for anger:

His mother didn't let him stay up. [What will he do next?] He'll kick his bed and hurt his toe.

This kind of logic appears again and again in the anger constructions offered by both females and males, ages 7 through 10.

It is still quite evident in the logic involved in 15-year-old female and male constructions for anger. The objects of anger and the actions linked to these objects, as described by ten 15-year-old females and ten 15-year-old males, are shown below:

FEMALES: (15% of the responses could not be categorized)

Object:	Fuss with peer (45%)	
Action:	*Dysfunctional Response*:	If it was real bad she'd probably go and cry
	Be Mad/Fight:	She would probably be angry for a long time
		Start a fight about it

		She'll probably be more mad at her friends and not call them for a long time
		Probably argue with her, won't talk to her for a few days
	Constructive Effort:	Go to the person ahead of her and try to change it
		Might try to make up
		Go up to the girl and ask her why she doesn't like what she's wearing
		Say something to them about it. Maybe they'll feel sorry

Object: Fuss with parents/teacher over autonomy (25%)

Action:	*Uncertain*:	Don't know
		Either go stomping off or apologize
	Assert Self:	Probably sass back
	Act Out:	Lock herself in her bedroom
		She will run away from home

Object: Must deal with a mess (15%)

Action:	*Just Do It*:	She'll clean it up
	Be Aggressive:	Hollered at them and made them help her clean it up
		Get mad at them and scold them

MALES: (13% of the responses could not be categorized)

Object: Fuss with peer (29%)

Action:	*Withdraw*:	He could walk away and forget about it because he's so mad
		If he was smart he'd let it pass; by then he wouldn't do it any more

Retaliate:		He could hit him or ask him who told him the information
		He'd get even with him, kick him in the shins
Object:	Peer's action violates rights (29%)	
Action:	*Passive Acceptance*:	It was probably the best thing for him
	Retaliate:	Look for the person who did it, stack their locker
		Feels like beating him up
		Hit him back or knock his books out of his hands
		They'll get in a fight; he'll get stolen thing back
Object:	Fuss with parents/teacher over autonomy (19%)	
Action:	*Passive Acceptance*:	He'll get three days suspension
		He'll just have to wait until he's old enough
	Act Out:	He ain't going to listen to his mom any more and might run away or something
Object:	Made bad grade (10%)	
Action:	*Become Afraid*:	His mom and dad are going to kill him
		He thinks his parents will get mad at him

As can be seen, forty-five percent of the female responses and fifty-eight percent of the male responses describe interactions with peers, and twenty-five percent and twenty-nine percent, respectively, describe interactions with parents or teachers. At this age, children's interactions with their peers are a very significant part of their social experience so many of their constructions for anger concern fusses with peers over rights and reputations.

It is also quite clear that these 15-year-olds, both female and male, are much more assertive with their peers than they are with their parents. The male constructions include considerable retaliation, much of it physical. Females, on the other hand, retaliate by not talking to the offending person. Some of the female anger constructions could be called constructive efforts to resolve the fuss while none of the male constructions are of this nature.

This small sample also includes one reason to be angry that the males do not mention—having to clean up a mess (made by siblings). Females then, appear to have some social experiences that males do not. They develop a logic for anger constructions that involves siblings (persons) younger than themselves with whom they have a caretaker relationship.

The following hypotheses are suggested by the three responses presented earlier and the data presented above:

1. Anger is not just anger transferred from one person to another. The anger constructions offered by these children suggest that they have one kind of anger with their peers and another kind of anger with their parents.

2. Children feel angry about different things. They feel angry when their rights and reputations are threatened in their relationships with their peers and when their autonomy is threatened in their relationships with their parents.

3. Children act upon these feelings in different ways, depending on the significant others involved. They are openly aggressive when angering with their peers. They are passively aggressive when angering with their parents.

   These constructions suggest that there are some unwritten rules for how one stands up for oneself when threatened by peers or parents. I suspect that such rules do, in fact, exist and that when we ask the second *why* question in the Emotional Development Interview (EDI) we will discover them. (See Chapter 5 for a description of the EDI.)

4. There appear to be gender differences in anger and even in the kinds of social experiences males and females have. Being expected to care for a younger sibling is a different social experience that must contribute to a particular logic for anger in these relationships.

But what can we say about the kind of discourse that children have had with their peers and their parents that contributed to these constructions? My data suggest a number of things about this discourse because children appear to talk to their parents about some of their feelings but not about others.

When angry with their parents, children say very little. They even appear to be afraid to let their parents see that they are angry. Any discourse is short-lived or it is non-verbal, so children act upon these feelings but typically they don't talk about them.

When angry with a sibling or a peer, children frequently talk to their parents or a teacher about it. They will mention what the sibling or peer has done, often in the form of a complaint. The parent or teacher must offer the child advice about what to do because children describe telling their parents or teachers about their angry feelings during this entire age period of 7 through 10.

Many children do not show anger toward their parents so there is little discourse. Although parents and teachers appear to advise children about how to act when angry with a sibling or a peer, they appear not to advise children how to act when angry with them. In fact, parents that do help children discuss their children's anger toward themselves are rare indeed, and this has ominous implications if the parents' actions toward their children are a frequent cause of the children's anger.

The logic of children's shame, guilt, sadness, pride, and happiness is also constructed in their heteronomous relationships with their parents (or caretakers), but there is a marked difference in these constructions when compared to the children's anger constructions. The logic of shame and guilt involves the feeling that one is "wrong" or "bad" or that one has done something "wrong" or "bad," but the appearance of shame and guilt constructions has some interesting complications.

Early in my efforts to talk with children about these two feelings, I discovered that before 7 or 8 years of age many children did not know what guilt was—the word had no meaning for them—but they did know what shame was. When I asked these children about feeling ashamed, they volunteered that they felt ashamed when they had done something "wrong" or "bad." Sometimes they would say, "I was bad." (At a later age, children begin to make a distinction between *being* wrong or bad and *doing* something wrong or bad, and this is a very important distinction.) Many of their guilt constructions included telling a parent that they had done something wrong, but this was not true for their shame constructions. Shame is apparently a feeling children keep to themselves, or is it that some parents shame their children and want them to suffer the shame for some reason?

On the other hand, it appears that many parents soon let their children know that they are criticizing the children's behavior and not the children themselves, because the children keep telling their parents about "getting in trouble" with teachers and others, apparently in an effort to get their parents' suggestions about what to do. If their parents were shaming them, I don't think they would continue to tell their parents about these incidents because feeling ashamed is typically acted upon by silence and an attempt to hide or cover up.

As an outcome of children's social experience shame and guilt become differentiated, but for many children they are still interrelated. I have seen children, and also some adults, who become very distressed whenever they do something wrong because they apparently regard this as just additional evidence that *they* are wrong or bad.

Some children's constructions for sadness were remarkable for one thing in particular—there was no mention of sharing this feeling with adults. Interestingly enough, very young children (up to age 7) felt sad in many of the same situations in which they also felt angry; this included their parents' or their peers' actions toward them. If angry in response to their parents' actions, they attempted to hide it. If angry at a peer, they might mention this to an adult, often as a complaint about the peer's action. But if they felt sad, they said nothing. This was very apparent in the sad constructions of some males and females, ages 7 through 15.

This phenomenon is illustrated by the following responses of Charlie, a 9-year-old male, who offered this construction for sad:

His friends let him down. [What will he do next?] He'd try to make new friends.

When I asked Charlie if he might be sad for any other reason, he offered the following constructions:

He hurt himself. [?] He'd go get a Band-Aid.

He did something bad and hurt someone. [?] He'd try to make it up.

He saw someone get hurt and it was his friend. [?] He'd go try to cheer them up.

One of his relatives died. [?] He'd feel sorry.

He saw all these other kids having fun but he wasn't having any fun. [?] He'd go inside and watch TV.

He lost a game. [?] He went into school and did his work.

When asked about anger, Charlie offered the following constructions:

Someone tripped him. [?] Go tell the teacher.

Someone punched him. [?] Go tell the teacher.

Someone he was playing with played with someone else. [?] He'd go get one of his other friends.

Someone took his bike—he'd feel angry and sad that someone took his bike. [?] He'd ask his mother for a new one, which she'd probably say no.

Someone hurt him. [?] Go tell the teacher.

Someone threw a rock at him. [?] Go tell the teacher.

A teacher yelled at him when he didn't do it. [?] He'd tell the teacher that he didn't do it.

If emotions are personal-social constructions, what are the rules some parents communicate to their children for what to do when they feel sad? My data suggest that we are not helping many children construct productive ways of acting when they feel sad because they have failed or have lost someone or something of value. It is as if it is shameful to ever feel sad. Is this why there is an increase in adolescent suicide?

Children's constructions for pride and happiness include many references to telling adults about their accomplishments and their good fortune. For the younger children (ages 7 through 10), parental largess, and parental permission and approval are frequently-mentioned reasons to feel happy. Later, when peers are more prominent as the significant others, their constructions for both pride and happiness include sharing these feelings with their peers. Both parents and peers, then, must help them decide how to act when they feel proud or happy.

The logic of children's feelings and emotions does appear to be constructed in the child-parent and the child-peer interaction and discourse. But when their feelings of shame and anger are in reaction to their parents' actions, there is little discourse initiated by the child and many children, when they feel sad for whatever reason, do not initiate much, if any, discourse.

When feeling angry, guilty, proud, or happy about situations involving their peers, or simply about their own accomplishments or good fortune, children do initiate discourse with their parents or other adults. They apparently share many of their feelings with both adults and peers, but they do not share some of their anger, shame, and sadness. The last is the most difficult to understand.

Gender differences, which are quite evident in children's constructions for anger, are also evident in their constructions for the other emotions. I predict that the use of the EDI, a longer interview in which more questions are asked, will produce data that reveal more pronounced gender differences.

As noted earlier, children do have discourse with their peers. As we all remember from our own experience in late childhood and adolescence, we develop friendships in which there is a great deal of sharing and discussion. There is also a lot of discourse with many other peers, and, as noted earlier, some of this discourse can be cruel and insensitive. Having a friend with whom one can talk about other peers' actions and comments can be helpful. Unfortunately, not all children develop friendships so their social experience will be limited and they will not have that discourse and discussion with others that is so vital to their emotional well-being and development.

DETERRENTS TO EMOTIONAL DEVELOPMENT

We are becoming increasingly aware of the kinds of social experiences that put our emotional development at risk. Interestingly enough, much of this new knowledge is being generated by those practicing the healing arts.

Let me review some of the social experiences now believed to be detrimental to our emotional development.

Dysfunctional Families and Emotional Neglect

Many families that appear to be healthy, happy families because there is no alcoholism, no physical abuse, no sexual abuse, and frequently not even any obvious conflict are nonetheless dysfunctional in that feelings and emotions are denied or ignored, and individual needs and values are ignored. Sometimes, parents quietly but persistently impose their own goals upon their children or they hold their children too close, treating them as their peers instead of as their children.

Some workaholic parents provide their children with a nice home, good schooling, expensive clothing, and financial support for their higher education, but neglect their children's emotional needs. The father and/or mother are always working and have little time to listen to their children talk about their interests, needs, and feelings. Typically, in the workaholic family, there are a number of subjects that just are not discussed. There is no abuse, just a benign neglect of needs, values, feelings, and emotions.

There are also families in which feelings are ignored or in which feelings are never expressed. If feelings exist at all, they are hidden or disguised. In such circumstances, some children simply fail to construct certain feelings and emotions. In their family it is not okay to be sad or angry; they are expected to always be happy, confident, and optimistic.

In some families, there is an injunction against having any feelings at all. Feelings are regarded as irrational and a departure from "manly" maturity. They are all right for women to have and to express, but not for men. In such a family situation, some children will simply not construct any but the most primitive feelings. They will feel good or bad and little else.

Children growing up in dysfunctional families are delayed or fixated in their emotional development, and there is usually a lack of balance to their development in that one or more feelings (shame, anger, or resentment) dominate their lives. In the context of the theory of emotional development I am advocating here, there is one question that can be asked to determine if a family is functional: Are all members of the family provided the opportunity to openly discuss their interests, needs, and feelings in a supportive atmosphere?

Physical Abuse

Physical abuse appears to foster a severe imbalance in emotional development; I am thinking especially of shame and anger. Many physically abused children develop a profound feeling of shame. They adapt to their abusive situations by embracing the belief that they deserve the abuse they are receiving because they are "bad." They appear to think, "I love my parents and they are good to me. I have a good home, nice clothes, and they feed me well. They do beat me, but it is because I am so bad."

Other children live with physical abuse for some time, probably believing that they deserve it. But then, by comparing themselves and their situations to those of their peers, they realize that something is terribly wrong and they become angry, even enraged or furious.

Both shame and anger, in the form of rage and fury, can be very unproductive because we attempt to assimilate all subjectively similar situations to these feelings. Our way of acting on these feelings, which proved to be adaptive in our families, is simply not adaptive in the world-at-large. And although we may be aware of what we are doing, we may not be even concretely conscious of the fact that this emotional behavior is not working for us. It is all we know to do. It should work, we believe, so we just try harder.

What is truly tragic is that many adults, abused as children, are walking time bombs when they themselves have children. The incidence of child abuse by parents who were themselves abused is very high.

It is probably not effective treatment to punish adults who abuse children. It may just confirm their belief that misbehavior must be punished and that the worse the misbehavior the more severe the punishment should be, which is the logic of abuse.

In our punishment of abusers then, we are caught up in a curious logic. What seems to occur is that even when their own abuse was feared and was responded to with rage, when they become parents and their children need to be disciplined, the only feeling they believe to be legitimate as a response to their children's misbehavior is rage. Unfortunately, physical violence is the only way that they know of acting on this feeling. This suggests that they were, and still are, identifying with their parents.

Someday public health policy may require that all adults who were abused as children accept the responsibility of seeking treatment before they have children of their own. This is a radical notion, but it would probably save many lives and put a stop to a lot of misery.

Sexual Abuse

As we become more open about sex in our society, and as sex and violence come to dominate the media, it should not surprise us that sexual harassment and sexual violence become more prevalent. While our increased openness may be a good thing, apparently we have not helped some members of our society value the feelings of belonging and mutuality nor have we helped them to become self-reflectively conscious of the positive feelings and emotions.

Sexual abuse appears to have devastating consequences. Almost without exception it produces a warp in the victim's emotional life. The victim often constructs a profound feeling of shame and depression.

How people feel about having been sexually abused as children often changes with age. Shame and depression, expressed by fearful, withdrawn behavior in which victims also feel helpless and hopeless, may be replaced by anger, resentment, and rage as they become older and have a different perspective on their childhood abuse or exploitation. These feelings may be expressed in both passive and active hostility, and aggressive "chip-on-the-shoulder" actions in social situations and interpersonal relationships. Needless to say, these feelings and emotions delay the development of emotional maturity.

Incest is an especially damaging experience. It can lead to all of the above plus an even more profound feeling of having been betrayed and exploited (Courtois, 1988). Shame and depression are frequently constructed as ways of dealing with incest. Because this experience may have begun as a not-too-unpleasant experience with people upon whom the children were dependent and for whom the children had considerable affection, especially strong feelings of shame and guilt that are very painful may later develop. Some children even feel that they were to blame for what happened, causing them to develop a self-hatred (Courtois, 1988).

As children become older, the belief that they were betrayed and exploited may contribute to a very strong rage. These feelings, and how people act on them, have serious consequences for their sense of well-being and their emotional maturity.

Alcohol and Narcotic Abuse

Many people abuse the use of alcohol and narcotics. They develop lifestyles that center on alcohol and drug abuse and, interestingly enough, when they decide to stop using these substances they feel lost. Breaking their dependency involves learning how to live and how to get on with their emotional development. I cannot imagine an emotionally mature substance abuser. The social experience of alcohol and narcotic abusers is simply not conducive to their emotional development. There is too much chaos, isolation, and denial.

It is not surprising that more and more adult children of alcoholics (ACOAs) are asking for treatment as they recognize that, as adults, they are facing social and emotional difficulties. It has been estimated that there are at least "22,000,000 people in the United States who are the grown offspring (age 18 or older) of parents who have had alcohol problems" (Vannicelli, 1989, p. 3).

Although there is controversy in the field over the growing number of generalizations about the characteristics of the ACOA population, it does seem clear that many, if not all, of them have had to contend with "inconsistent parenting, with unpredictable rules and limits; chaotic or tense family environments; poor communication, with unclear messages and broken promises; and loneliness and isolation, as family members attempt to hide the family's problems and reduce the potential for shame and embarrassment" (Vannicelli, 1989, pp. 6–7).

The difficulties that show up rather consistently in the growing body of literature on the characteristics and treatment of ACOAs are: (a) difficulties with interpersonal relationships, (b) lack of trust in others, and (c) denial of feelings.

My belief is that the feelings and emotions constructed by children growing up in alcoholic families enable the children to adapt and to survive in these family situations, but that they prove to be maladaptive in the world-at-large. This must also be true of growing up in a family where there is narcotic abuse. In my clinical experience, some ACOAs deny having any feelings at all. Others lead lives distorted by anger or shame.

It seems clear that abusing alcohol and narcotics, and being the child of an adult who does so, is conducive to delayed emotional development. Vannicelli (1989) reminds us, however, that there is increasing evidence that many ACOAs may grow up to be well-adjusted, "perhaps, *because of* the coping skills they have developed" (p. 9).

It would be interesting to make a comparative study of the emotional development of a group of well-adjusted ACOAs and a group of poorly adjusted ACOAs. I believe that a number of interesting differences would be found.

Emotional Abuse

Love (1990) has called our attention to another kind of emotional experience that distorts and/or delays emotional development. She describes the experience of being the chosen child and being treated like a peer rather than like a child as having serious consequences for emotional well-being. Some parents need their child to be their pal or their best friend and confidant while the child is still much too young to manage such a relationship. All too often, these parents try to use the child to meet their own needs and they ignore the child's needs.

Put in this position, these children may be overwhelmed and feel guilty that they cannot be more helpful and protective, or they develop a very exaggerated sense of their position and power. Both ways of responding can lead to feelings and emotions that are maladaptive outside the parent-child relationship.

This syndrome is not rare; I have seen it in my own clinical practice. It does appear to delay emotional maturity. The children have to struggle with their enmeshment and literally fight to become autonomous.

Being Exceptional

Exceptional children are at risk to have delayed or retarded emotional development. Our society has made remarkable progress in its acceptance of exceptional children and adults. All schools now have procedures to identify children with special needs, and they modify the curriculum to help meet these special needs.

But, as I have described elsewhere (Dupont, 1978), the back-to-basics emphasis on academic achievement and a special plan for each child often ignores the child's need to have a peer group that encourages reciprocity and mutuality. The exaggerated competitiveness and the rigid conformity that is often dominant in preadolescence and early adolescence can have devastating consequences for the exceptional child.

Being too small, too tall, too thin, or too obese can lead to rejection, isolation, shame, and depression. The cruel teasing she endured for being too tall led one Atlanta girl to commit suicide (she shot herself in the face!). They called her "stick" and "tree" and told her she would never have a boyfriend because she was too ugly (Dupont, 1989).

However, it is not being different in itself that is the source of the difficulty, but the way that difference interferes with the social experience that is so essential to emotional development. Surely there is apt to be a feeling of shame, that is, of being very different if not profoundly different than others, that must be alleviated or changed, if possible. With acceptance and appropriate social experience, this can be achieved. Unfortunately, this does not just happen naturally. Normal children may be uncomfortable with children that are different, especially if they interact with these different children in a stress-laden competitive situation.

Surely the new emphasis on cooperative learning is helpful for all exceptional children, but the optimal development of deformed children and some physically handicapped children requires a special plan to provide these children with the social experience so essential to their emotional development. My point here is that the need for social experience is often poorly understood and, consequently, social experience is not systematically provided by our society.

Courtois (1988) also reminds us that children and adults with physical and emotional disabilities and limitations are at high risk for sexual abuse:

Recent school and clinical reports substantiate that children and adults with limitations constitute a population at risk for sexual abuse. . . . Physical or emotional differences and disabilities often make these individuals more vulnerable to victimization, less able to protect themselves, and less likely to receive adequate social services. . . . [And] in some cases, disability or damage may have resulted either directly or indirectly from the abuse or the abuse may have caused additional disability. (pp. 281–282)

Trauma

Ed Bradley of the CBS-TV program "60 Minutes" recently reviewed a brief therapy program at the 102nd Street School located in the Watts area of Los Angeles. The program was for children who had experienced the death of a parent, sibling, or other relative in a violent, senseless incident, typically a shoot-out of some kind on the streets of Watts.

These children had been shocked into a traumatic stress syndrome by their experience. Several of them were essentially numb and speechless; they could not talk or function normally. The school principal, counselor, and psychologist felt that without a special therapeutic program these children would be damaged for life. This prediction is consistent with the theory of emotional development I am presenting here.

There are, of course, many other reports and case histories illustrating the effect that trauma has on emotional development.

The Absence of an Empathic Nurturing Relationship

There appears to be an increasing number of children who do not have an empathic nurturing relationship with even one person. Many of their basic needs are not being met consistently, if at all. This situation is very threatening to their well-being if not their very survival, and it triggers a wired-in, highly energized reaction to a perceived threat.

In infancy, their reaction is a crying that is easily recognized as rage along with an increase in activity level that is random and unproductive. With maturation and social experience, the actions that become linked to rage include self-mutilation and an effort to hurt others. These rage constructions are often pure action level constructions with no self-reflective consciousness involved. As one 10-year-old male reported: "Yeah, I feel angry." [Why?] "Because I'm angry." [What do you do then?] "I hurt somebody."

An increasing number of children appear to be constructing feelings of rage that they are acting out in violence. This violence is becoming an epidemic.

SUMMARY

Let me try to fit the essence of the growing literature into the theoretical context I am developing here. As I see it, all too often children growing up in dysfunctional families, children subject to abuse, and many exceptional children develop negative feelings about themselves, significant others, and their lives. They then develop habitual ways of acting on these feelings that are adaptive in their current situations but ineffective and unproductive in the world-at-large.

These feelings and emotions are often constructed early, before language (perhaps as feelings and action schemes). They are not cognized and reflected upon, that is, they are never talked about— they are just ignored, tolerated, disguised, or denied.

Some children develop a profound feeling of shame, sometimes for both themselves and their families, and they assimilate many other people, events, and situations into these shame constructions. Hence, they are passive, avoidant, and even apologetic to many other people and in many situations.

Others develop rage, contempt, or resentment constructions into which they assimilate many of the people, events, and situations that they encounter. The feelings and emotions the children construct to give them some sense of well-being in whatever situation they have grown up in prove to be nonfunctional when they enter new situations (as is inevitable).

Since they have never developed the habit or practice of talking about their feelings and how they act upon them, thereby creating emotions, they are stuck and they flounder. They continue to have mostly negative feelings about themselves and many events and situations, and to have poor interpersonal relationships.

They need, of course, to clarify, modify, refine, or construct new feelings and new ways of acting upon these feelings, thus constructing new emotions. They cannot do this alone because they are not conscious of either their feelings or their actions, even in concrete terms, nor can they think about their feelings and emotions in abstract self-reflection. Without help, emotional maturity is difficult to achieve.

There is one other deterrent to emotional development that I have encountered in my professional experience. Some people are handicapped by the unsound, sometimes even weird ways of thinking about their feelings and emotions that they have acquired in their families, in previous counseling or psychotherapy, in self-help groups, or in the self-help literature.

For example, many people have picked up the notion that they need to express their anger more aggressively or it will build up and then they will explode. Or, they have learned to believe that they must control their anger or their temper and they are trying to do just that, rather than learning more effective ways of managing the situations in which they anger. Our theories about our emotions are an important element of our consciousness and they must be sound or our well-being will suffer.

Since emotional development is a product of our social experience, we are perhaps wise to be concerned about this generation of children because there does appear to be a breakdown in much of our social fabric. For too many children, an empathic nurturing environment is simply not there.

I find myself concerned that although we seem to be increasingly knowledgeable about the factors that deter emotional development, we are giving relatively little attention to the kinds of experiences that stimulate and facilitate emotional development. Some children achieve a high level of emotional maturity in spite of very adverse circumstances. Perhaps we should study these children.

5

Applications

There are tens of millions of emotionally handicapped children and adults in our society who need help, aren't getting it, and, as things stand, never will get it. (Albee, 1993, p. 88)

One person can help another to become more of a person. (Shotter, 1984, p. 49)

In the course of our emotional development, we construct and reconstruct feelings and ways of acting on these feelings (emotions) to manage the issues that arise in our interactions with others. There is remarkable agreement about why these issues are significant for our well-being. Between fifty and seventy percent of children at a particular age will suggest the same reasons for feeling angry, ashamed, guilty, sad, proud, or happy. They appear to feel angry when confronted by some psychological threat, ashamed when their differences are exposed and devalued, guilty when they have done the wrong thing or harmed others, and sad when they have failed or lost someone or something of value. They feel proud when they achieve something against the odds and happy when they are doing well and all is going well.

These are just some of the contingencies about which a common understanding is shared. There must be many more. At maturity, our feelings and emotions have much in common—they serve the self, they are an effective way of confronting and managing life's vicissitudes, and they meet our needs.

But our development is characterized by changing needs. Our needs in infancy are different than our needs in adolescence and adulthood. As new needs arise our feelings change, and we construct new ways of acting upon these feelings thereby constructing new emotions to mediate our interactions with evermore complicated events, situations, and different significant others. Our needs become values as we learn to value what helps us to create a stable, but flexible, personal and social equilibrium.

The changes and transformations that our maturation and newly acquired needs move us to make are a product of our social experience and the feedback we get as an element of that experience. They are also facilitated by our evolving consciousness. We depend upon inborn feeling-action constructions for our survival, but through the processes of assimilation and accommodation these inborn constructions become elaborated into a complex system of feelings and emotions that serve our adaptation and equilibrium.

Our consciousness not only makes us aware, but it becomes what is, at first, an intuitive "know how" and then a concrete personal-social intelligence and later an abstract, complex, and flexible personal-social intelligence that is self-reflective in nature. We become an object of our own consciousness and we become conscious of our feelings. We can verbalize, examine, and reconstruct our feelings. We become conscious of the actions through which we express our feelings and the probable consequences of these actions. At maturity, we have a rich system of values and a rich repertoire of feelings and emotions.

It is important to recognize that in our acquisition of that system of shared meaning that is our culture, we move toward conformity and then toward autonomy. It is only after we have internalized the values and injunctions of our culture that in response to our unique interests, abilities, and skills, we can develop a unique and autonomous identity. Before we internalize the values and standards of our culture, we are in alienation and in continual conflict with that culture. We become free and autonomous when we embrace the best our culture has to offer and then transcend it.

But our autonomy is never complete and total. We also appear to need mutuality in our relationships—a mutuality that is always in dynamic tension with our apparent need for autonomy. And gender makes a difference. For females, "movement into connections and relationships is the primary element of growth" (Jordan, 1993). In my experience, growth in competence and autonomy appears to be more highly valued by males. This suggests that the goals of development, of emotional education, and of psychotherapy are different for females than they are for males.

But as with our growth into conformity and then away from it, maybe females and males first need to develop a distinctive gender identity and then move toward an identity that integrates the need for competence, autonomy, and mutuality in some meaningful way. It is my impression that females in our culture are making more progress in achieving this kind of identity than are males. So many males appear to be insecure and defensive about their bonding and their "male" identities.

Would activities in which children have an opportunity to understand and appreciate both their needs and those of children with other gender identities be helpful? Would an earlier and longer emphasis on empathy for both self and others also be helpful? I believe it would be, and that we should try to provide our children with just such experiences.

This is a new way of looking at our feelings and emotions, and it has implications for the assessment of emotional development, emotional education, and psychotherapy.

ASSESSING EMOTIONAL DEVELOPMENT

In the preceding chapters, I have alluded again and again to an interview procedure used to gather information about our feelings and emotions. The content and procedures followed in this interview have evolved in parallel with the crystallization of the theory of emotional development I am presenting herein. It could, however, be described as an application of this neo-Piagetian theory to the assessment of emotional development.

As Berk (1989) suggests, our theories of child development "tell us what aspects of child behavior are important to observe" (p. 5). In this theory, there are several elements in our consciousness (which Piaget regards as behavior) that we wish to observe, namely, our feelings and emotions. And since these two elements of our consciousness are regarded as constructions and not as innate, we also want to observe all of the elements that contribute to them as constructions. This includes the needs and values that inform our feelings (as energy-regulating evaluations) and the value-informed actions we choose to restore our equilibrium.

What is needed then, is some "experiential X ray" (Weiner, et al., 1977) that puts these elements and processes into a coherent picture for all to see. It is in response to this need that the Emotional Development Interview (EDI) evolved.

The EDI focuses on six emotions. (Other emotions can be added, of course.) For the four "negative" emotions (anger, shame, guilt, and sadness), it involves asking six questions and whatever follow-up questions are needed to provide an understanding of the situation in which the subject feels angry, ashamed, guilty, or sad; the subject's reasons for feeling that way; what the subject does when feeling that way; and the reasons for doing whatever he or she does when feeling that way. In the sixth question, the subject is asked how it all turns out and if this is the way he or she wanted it to turn out.

The EDI is modified somewhat for the two "positive" emotions (pride and happiness) and involves asking five questions. The first four questions are the same as those for the negative emotions, but since pride and happiness are desirable affective states, the subject is asked in the fifth question if he or she ever deliberately does anything to feel proud or happy. Many children and some adults believe that pride and happiness just happen and some people believe that it is wrong to try to feel proud or happy. If this is true, it is valuable information about the person.

When interviewing children age 10 and younger, I have found it helpful to use a series of pictures of boys and girls whose facial expressions are representative of the six feelings. The feeling is named and the EDI questions are asked about the child in the picture; for example, "Here is a picture of a boy (or girl) like you who is feeling angry. Why is he/she feeling that way?" and so forth.

Using the pictures turns the interview into a projective interview, but it has proven to be an effective way to help young children talk about their feelings and emotions.

The EDI is conducted as an interview and not as if one is filling out a questionnaire. Asking *why* can be challenging and even confrontational. This is to be avoided if possible, so I often inquire about subjects' reasons for their feelings or their actions in this way: "Help me to understand why that seemed threatening to you," or "Help me to understand why that action seemed like the thing to do."

Some children and immature adults can describe what they do, but they have difficulty answering the *why* questions. They cannot reflect upon their own feelings and actions, so in answer to the *why* questions they will just repeat their description of *when* they were angry, ashamed, guilty, or sad, as if the description, itself, is also the explanation. Some adults will do something similar to this: They will say, "I've always felt that way," and "I've done that since my childhood when my parents ignored me," as if the history of their feelings and actions is also an explanation of why they feel and act as they do. These responses indicate where the subjects are in their emotional development.

The EDI questions require subjects to think about things that most of them have not been thinking about and to recognize that they have choices that they did not realize they had. This is why many subjects will express surprise at the end of an EDI interview. "Gee, that was interesting!" they will say, as if they had learned something new about themselves.

In conducting the EDI, interviewers will realize that the questions they are asking encourage subjects to cognize their experience and to become more conscious of what they are feeling and doing. This is also the essence of psychotherapy so interviewers will respond to subjects' answers with empathy, knowing that the EDI is, in fact, a mini-therapy session. This is, of course, the very reason that the EDI is so potentially powerful. It puts assessment on the same continuum as treatment.

Subjects' responses in the EDI will provide the following information:

1. Their level of consciousness;

2. The identity of their significant others and how they are relating to them;

3. Profiles of their development of anger, shame, guilt, sadness, pride, and happiness, and, if appropriate, other emotions as well and;

4. The needs and values that are currently dominant in their lives.

The information obtained with the EDI can be used to study any number of hypotheses about emotional development. For example, I would like to obtain new interview data from a wide age range of children and adults to increase our understanding of this important domain of development. Also, seniors' feelings and emotions appear to be different but we have little understanding of just how they are different.

And there is, of course, the gender issue. Wouldn't interviews at a sequence of different ages provide us with information that would give us a much better understanding of how the development of feelings and emotions is similar and different for males and females? Are there males or females who are more like the other gender than their own? Will some males and females share the same needs and values and, therefore, have the same kinds of feelings and emotions? Are there large scale differences that suggest we need two developmental models, one for males and one for females?

I regard what I have presented thus far as just a beginning of a work that could be in progress for some time. Even with our current knowledge, however, the information obtained with the EDI can also be used to formulate treatment plans. It can be especially useful when, for whatever reason, treatment must be time-limited. For children, it suggests who might be included in the treatment plan. For both children and adults, it shows in bold relief what feelings, relationships, and situations they should be encouraged to talk about further. Thus, the EDI paves the way for an easy transition into play therapy or psychotherapy; however, its greatest value may be its use as a research tool.

EMOTIONAL EDUCATION

There is abundant evidence that we take emotional development for granted. For the most part we regard it as something that just happens. We see it essentially as an independent variable. Thus, retarded emotional development, emotional immaturity, poor impulse control, and so forth are used to explain a person's inappropriate social behavior and many other kinds of pathological behavior.

But perhaps we should look at emotional development as a dependent variable and emotional maturity as a desirable educational and social objective. To do this, we must give up the idea that our emotions are innate and just transferred from one object to another. We must also abandon the idea that one of our emotions—anger—is innate and located in our unconscious where it must be kept and carefully controlled. I believe that this hypothesis, extended to many other emotions as well, has led us to believe that it is only in treatment that we can affect our emotional maturity and that education has no role.

Throughout this book I have argued that our emotions, as suggested by Piaget, are better regarded as constructions that are acquired in the course of our development, and that they undergo considerable change in the course of that development.

There is a program in Hawaii called "Healthy Start" that appears to verify the hypothesis that our emotions are constructions. In this program, new mothers who are identified as high risk to become abusers are provided with a family support worker to give them systematic emotional support and instruction in child care. The incidence of child abuse has been dramatically reduced by this program.

This unique education program prevents the construction of the frustration-anger abuse syndrome that might otherwise develop in these mother-child interactions (where the mother is considered to be high risk for abuse by virtue of the fact that she is, for example, young, single, and lacking in family support).

The anger (frustration-anger in this case) is not assumed to be in the mother but rather to arise (be constructed) in the mother-child interactions under certain conditions. Certainly this kind of effort makes much more sense than to punish or treat the mother and the child, often years later, because of the abuse.

This program also illustrates what is for me the most basic principle of emotional education, namely, that we help people learn how to deal more effectively not with their feelings and emotions but rather with those situations that are the objects of their feelings and emotions.

The notions that our emotions are personal constructions always acquired in a social context; that feelings are energy-regulating evaluations of events, situations, and objects (usually people); that we construct our consciousness by cognizing our experience and that there is a distinctive logic for each of our respective emotions that is transformed in the normal course of development—and that this logic is always informed by our needs and values as we confront the psychosocial issues inevitable in our interaction with our culture—all of these notions, I believe, make emotional education a feasible enterprise.

Early Emotional Education

Emotional education begins in the family, be it one parent or two, or it begins in the child's early relationships with caretakers. It begins as early as the first year of life and is definitely in progress during the second and third years of life. Dunn and Brown (1991) observed it in process as early as 18 months, and it appears to be deliberate, not just natural, because they observed large differences in the way parents facilitate the process.

In a review of their own research and that of others on the control and regulation of emotions beginning as early as 18 months, Dunn and Brown (1991) identified four processes that appear to be involved in children's early emotional development: (a) their development of language; (b) their discourse with their parents about affective states, their own and others; (c) their observations of others' affective states; and (d) their pretend play focusing on affective states or feelings and their meaning for them.

Let me describe in more detail what I think Dunn and Brown (1991) have discovered. With the development of language, children begin to acquire words that add a conceptual dimension to their discourse with others. They comment to their caretakers about their affective states, typically some need, and they ask for help. They also ask questions about others' affective states and soon use this knowledge to achieve some goal. In their second and third years, they may even try to disguise these affective states to achieve some end they have in mind. They develop likes and dislikes and, aware of others' distress, they may use both words and actions to provide comfort to them. There is also interaction and discourse with siblings and peers, so having siblings and peers can be an important factor in children's emotional development.

Dunn and Brown (1991) discuss these observations with reference to the development of affect regulation in early childhood. As mentioned in Chapter 1, I believe that what they are observing are children's very acts of constructing their feelings and emotions in their interactions with their parents, caretakers, siblings, and peers.

The linking of affective states and their causes (and the words that parents or caretakers provide to children in their discourse) is the crucial step in the transformation of affective states into feelings, which are also concepts, and this process is a vital step in children's language and emotional development. These words for feelings not only label and categorize affective states, but they also imply a cause and are, therefore, a part of the shared meaning of the culture in which these events are taking place.

Early in the process of construction, affective states are purely situational; there is no conservation of feeling from one situation to the next. Late in the process of construction, feelings are conserved from one situation to the next in the child's language for feelings and emotions, and the child's life is different from this point on. These acts of construction and reconstruction, through which the meaning we share in our culture increasingly provides structure for our emotional life, are the critical factors in our emotional development.

What this suggests to me is that, from time to time, as the meaning we share with others in our culture is enlarged, we may become sensitive to entirely new values or nuances of values, leading us to new evaluations of events and, thus, to the construction of new feelings (and to new words for our vocabulary). Then, too, as our understanding of the meaning we share with others in our culture grows, we may reconstruct the logic of those constructions we have already acquired. In this instance, the logic (or structure) of a particular feeling or emotion we have already categorized and labeled will be transformed.

Thus, the logic of anger, shame, guilt, sadness, pride, and happiness goes through a series of transformations as development proceeds toward maturity. Almost certainly, we construct many other feelings and emotions in this same way. We must recognize that this process of constructing feelings—this linkage of affective states to causes and then to labels, thus creating feelings and emotions—can be a lifelong process.

This process begins early, and two important differences appear early as well. There are large individual differences in family discourse that are correlated with children's affective perspective-taking abilities three and four years later (Dunn & Brown, 1991). This suggests, quite simply, that in families where feelings are attended to and talked about, emotional development is facilitated; in families where feelings are not attended to or talked about at all, emotional development is delayed or retarded.

Dunn and Brown (1991) also observed gender differences in the parent-child discourse and children's affective perspective-taking abilities three and four years later; Paley (1984) observed gender differences in the way boys and girls played in kindergarten; and gender differences were apparent in the data I collected from subjects ages 7 through 25. Females in this age range appeared to be more concerned about feelings, reputations, and relationships, and males appeared to be more concerned about rules, possessions, competition, and achievement. It is not surprising that these early-appearing differences will also be evident many years later in male and female feelings and emotions, but as we now realize this is a complicated matter and one that certainly deserves further study.

I would argue that emotional development is a product of emotional education. It is not just something that occurs naturally, but it is a manifestation of parental and caretaker values. It is promulgated by parents and caretakers who regard children as not just something to be tended to, but as children who are becoming human beings in relationship to themselves, and so they listen to their children's comments and questions and respond to their children deliberately to nurture their development—or they ignore them for one reason or another and the children adapt to this neglect, however benign, as best they can.

One way children adapt to being neglected or abused is by constructing anger or rage, and we certainly seem to have more of this than ever before. Another way many children respond to neglect and abuse is to develop feelings of shame and helplessness, which are often present in depression.

There is a very strong probability that these serious differences in emotional well-being and emotional maturity, which are evident early and then again in adolescence and adulthood, begin in the family and, with increasing frequency, in the child's preschool experiences in day care and early education. In the 1990 census, it was found that fifty-three percent of the mothers with children under one year of age were in the labor force. Among mothers who were college graduates and had a child under one year of age, sixty-eight percent were working (Eckholm, 1992). More and more children are spending longer hours in day care and early education programs.

With the demise of the family as the crucible of emotional development, parents and primary caretakers are increasingly forced to share responsibility for their children's development with others (for example, day care personnel, teachers, coaches, and other mentors). This is simply a fact of life. Our tendency to deny this makes me anxious and I have to act on that anxiety, which is what I am doing right now.

It seems to me that we must extend the emotional education that has been initiated in the earliest parent-child interaction into the day care experience and the rest of the child's early educational experience. This appears to be especially important in view of the fact that so many mothers with a child under one year of age are now working.

Surely it makes sense to train parents, caretakers, and teachers to respond to children's comments and questions about feelings and the function of these feelings in human relationships. I believe that we should also make talking about feelings in relationships a selected component in the day care and early education curriculum.

In these early educational experiences, we can extend and enlarge upon the activities that Dunn and Brown (1991) observed to be influential in children's early emotional development: (a) observing feelings in others' relationships; (b) talking with caretakers or teachers about their feelings and asking about others' feelings; and (c) having role-playing experiences that focus on needs, feelings, and their actions upon these feelings.

Emotional Education in Elementary and Middle School

As the age of the children increases, discourse which may consist of comments and responses to questions may become genuine discussion and, eventually, dialogue. We can provide children with age-appropriate interactions involving needs and feelings in the form of cartoons to observe, sequences of pictures to discuss, and stories to listen to or read and discuss. We could even produce age-appropriate television dramas for children to view and discuss, and we could provide age-appropriate role-taking opportunities for them, including the opportunity to write, produce, and act in dramas of their own creation.

I believe that most of the affective, psychological, and character education programs that are presently available to counselors and teachers, for use with children K-12, should give an even more deliberate emphasis to the development of a repertoire of effective and constructive feelings and emotions. We now have the theoretical foundation for programs that have this emphasis. These programs would focus on two interdependent goals: (a) the achievement of a self-reflective level of consciousness, and (b) the acquisition of a repertoire of value-informed and effective feelings and emotions. The methods used would be elaborations of the processes identified by Dunn and Brown (1991).

Method 1. Participants would be provided ample opportunity to observe, read about, and hear about others who are in the process of confronting and responding to the identity or well-being issues which, in our culture, are the core issues for anger, shame, guilt, sadness, pride, and happiness.

Both the projective procedures used by my colleagues and I in our earlier work and the EDI have provided us with numerous examples of the kinds of situations and events that children believe to embody these issues. And, as we know, the events and situations about which children feel angry, ashamed, guilty, and so forth are somewhat different at each age level. Therefore, the materials the children are provided to observe, read about, or listen to would involve different events and situations depending on the age of the participants. Children would then be provided the opportunity to discuss the needs, feelings, actions, and values of both male and female central characters.

These materials would provide children with many real-life mini-dramas presented through several modalities so that children with hearing or visual disabilities could also react to them and then participate in a discussion of them. The teacher/counselor presenting these materials would also guide the children's discussion and serve as a consultant when necessary.

Method 2. Children would be invited to share their experience with these six feelings and emotions (anger, shame, guilt, sadness, pride, and happiness) and other emotions, if deemed desirable. This would be done in the EDI format and in groups of eight to twelve, if possible, because this is the optimal size group for this kind of activity.

Although children would be asked to share their experiences with these feelings and emotions, the focus of the discussion would not be on learning to control or regulate them—doing this would repeat the substantialist fallacy—but rather on finding more effective ways to deal with the situations in which they feel angry, ashamed, guilty, and so forth. We do not want to help children deal with their "anger" or their "guilt"; we want to help them respond more effectively and productively to the situations in which they feel angry or guilty. We want to help them construct effective and productive emotions. This is probably the most important insight that my neo-Piagetian theory provides for us.

Method 3. Children would be invited to create their own mini-dramas and role-playing opportunities. This would be an elaboration of the pretend play observed by Dunn and Brown (1991).

The creation of these plots and scripts could be fun and a most valuable experience for children at all age levels. It would help them to achieve a healthy distance from some of these vital issues, a distance that might help them to achieve a perspective where a self-reflective consciousness is more easily acquired and maintained. I believe that these goals and methods and this content emphasis could be used to create emotional education programs for all age levels. They are very similar to those employed in *Toward Affective Development* (Dupont, Gardner, & Brody, 1974) and *Transition* (Dupont & Dupont, 1979). These two programs have been used extensively by both teachers and counselors.

My hope is that this theory of emotional development will enable teachers and counselors to conduct these activities with more confidence that what they are doing is both valuable and psychologically sound. The individual counseling they provide to children in emergency situations is certainly necessary, but deliberately planned emotional education activities can contribute to the emotional development of all students and not just those with acute needs.

Some time ago I began employing this new way of thinking about emotions and their construction and function in my professional practice. I tested it in anger workshops for middle school students and for teachers of various grade levels. The EDI questions provided the structure for the workshops for both the middle school students and the teachers. These workshops received very positive evaluations.

Conducting these workshops led me to the conclusion that all caretakers, teachers, social workers, counselors, psychologists, and administrators working with students at all levels, from preschool through college, would profit from at least one course in emotional development. This would provide them with a basic understanding of how feelings and emotions are constructed and how they mediate our experiences with our social world.

These professionals would also profit from at least one semester of emotional education in which they become conscious of their own anger, shame, guilt, sadness, pride, and happiness constructions, thereby gaining an understanding of how these constructions influence their everyday experience. Yes, this course would probably make some of them aware that they need psychotherapy, and this is as it should be. Our children deserve emotionally mature human beings as the guardians of their emotional development.

Children in Trauma

Should I call what I am about to discuss psychotherapy or emotional education? I am not sure. Perhaps it is both. But helping children who have had traumatic experiences is important. It may even be critical for their emotional development.

Let us return our attention to the children in Watts who had witnessed the violent death of a parent or sibling. Working with these children in small groups and providing them with the opportunity to share their experiences through drawings, paintings, and discussion appears to have been helpful. Why?

Before sharing their experiences, many of these children behaved as if they were in shock. They were withdrawn and uncommunicative. It was as if they simply were not dealing with what had happened and were unclear about how they felt about it; hence, they were psychologically immobilized. They were holding the experience "out there," so to speak. They had to cognize the experience by taking it in and dealing with it—to feel sad and to grieve, and in the process, to integrate the experience into the rest of their ongoing lives.

Those working with these children were supportive and encouraging while inviting the children to share and to face their loss, to be sad, to grieve, and then to reconstruct their lives. They knew the children could not reverse their loss, but they believed that they could help them relate to and integrate the experience, which is what they did. This is why it worked.

Children face other traumas, most of them not as dramatic, but traumatic nonetheless. These traumas include divorce, illness, injury, failure, and, of course, neglect, and physical and sexual abuse. Many schools have group counseling or emotional education programs for abused children and children of divorce. For reasons similar to those discussed above, these programs can be very helpful.

Illness, injury, and failure, especially a public failure, can also be very traumatic. We appear to recognize that children (and adults as well) who have serious life-threatening or terminal illnesses, such as cancer or AIDS, need help relating to their illnesses, as do their parents, relatives, and friends. How people feel about illness, their own or others', is a critical factor in how they relate to the illness. The opportunity to talk about it, to take it in, to clarify their feelings about it, and to then decide how they are going to relate to it are critical factors for their recovery and their emotional development.

Injuries can be traumatic as well. We all know how emotionally traumatic serious sports injuries can be. The media have made us aware of this. What we often do not recognize is that even minor injuries, when not discussed and when poorly understood, can lead to very damaging consequences.

Failure, especially public failure, can be very devastating. As I have noted, children tend to hide or deny feeling sad or depressed. Wouldn't it be wise to include failure and loss in the emotional education curriculum and/or wouldn't it be wise to offer sadness and depression workshops to middle school and high school students? In my opinion, over time, the public's mental health could be improved considerably by these kinds of emotional education activities.

Juvenile Violence Prevention Programs

In Chapter 4, I described how children who do not have an empathic nurturing relationship with even one other person are at high risk to develop rage constructions that involve acting out against themselves or others in violent and destructive behavior.

In Hawaii, health professionals were able to identify mothers who were at risk to become involved in child abuse. With a concentrated effort, children at high risk to become violent could probably be identified as well. There are almost certainly a number of personal and social indicators that could be used to identify these children. As mentioned, the absence of even one person providing the child with an empathic nurturing relationship is probably one indicator; there must be others.

Having identified these children, we could then design programs to help them meet their needs. Maybe they need an empathic nurturing mentor. Maybe they would become less prone to violence if everyone they encountered in the school and in the criminal justice system was more empathic and nurturing rather than angry at them and "hard-nosed." Maybe our anger at them is not an effective and productive anger.

Comments

There is an element of irony in what I believe to be true of emotional education. The popular notion that we must be autonomous, especially as this need is demonstrated by males in our culture, is totally at odds with what we now know about how we become emotionally mature. The notion that our needs and feelings are uniquely ours and not like anyone else's and are, therefore, to be kept as closely guarded secrets is antithetical to emotional maturity and to everyone's well-being. Our first challenge, then, may be to do what we can to modify this deeply-rooted male fixation on being the strong, silent, "I'll handle this myself," unfeeling, macho man.

We do want to accept, respect, and even celebrate personal and cultural differences, but perhaps we should honor and appreciate our similarities. We are, after all, more alike than different. Our goal should be "intersubjectively shared understandings . . . made and agreed upon by people working in dialogue together" (Shotter, 1975, p. 135).

When emotional education is not provided or when it fails, psychotherapy is often necessary.

PSYCHOTHERAPY

To a considerable extent, we can meet our clients' immediate needs for constancy, comfort, and empathy. We can provide a relationship in which we are constant in our presence and attention, we can provide a comfortable place for us to talk, and we can assure our clients that, within limits, what they talk to us about is confidential. And we can be empathic, but as Jordan (1993) reminds us, that empathy is always imperfect. However, I have come to believe that my empathic effort to understand my clients is the most important thing that I do as a therapist.

More recently, I have come to believe that the *structure* that I provide to my clients' consciousness by my questions is the second most important thing that I do as a therapist. Many readers may be surprised at this statement, believing that therapists do not impose structure on their clients' consciousness. I sincerely believe that this is an illusion, and that in the course of our development and socialization we increasingly acquire a system of shared meaning with the other human beings with whom we share a culture. Indeed, many people eventually transcend their culture, but we become human beings within a culture created by other human beings, and the structure of our consciousness reflects the prevailing values of that culture.

The questions we ask our clients help them to achieve a self-reflective consciousness that facilitates their socialization and their personal and interpersonal equilibrium. The questions I ask are essentially the same as those included in the EDI. Although I may ask them in many different ways, they are always in my mind during my discussion and dialogue with my clients.

This is consistent with the two major objectives I pursue in my clinical practice: (a) to help clients achieve a self-reflective consciousness, and (b) to help clients develop more mature feelings and emotions. I have found these objectives to be appropriate for all of my work, in both time-limited therapy and long-term therapy.

Many clients present themselves with an essentially healthy self, but they are currently caught up in something that they do not understand, are anxious about, and feel they need help with. Other clients present themselves with real disorders of the self (Elson, 1987). They need a long-term, empathic relationship with a therapist who can be a self-object for them. This therapist must have feelings and emotions they can emulate and internalize as their own.

Needless to say, with what appears to be an increase in clients with narcissistic disorders the therapist often has to handle a lot of self-protective denial, avoidance, and withdrawal if progress is to be made. Once a good working alliance has been established, it is necessary to be very confrontational in the face of some of these self-protective maneuvers. If this is not done, the therapy can go on forever.

What is meaningful to me is this. Most people that seek psychological assistance are delayed in their emotional development. They are often operating at a very concrete level of consciousness, which results in their being very inflexible and maladapted to their current circumstances. Some have long-standing personality disorders so that their lives are dominated by one or two emotions, often anger or shame and, occasionally, depression, or some combination of these three. They are oblivious to their needs and they have an impoverished system of values which means, as I have suggested earlier, that they are unfeeling as well.

Again and again, I have discovered that there will be two or three defining experiences that were turning points in their lives. The feelings and emotions they constructed to deal with these experiences have set the tone for the rest of their lives. They assimilate most of their current experiences to these defining experiences and are, therefore, stuck with some way of adapting that was effective earlier in their lives but that is ineffective now. They will often return to those experiences again and again in their therapy. This can be helpful because, with each reconstruction of the experience, they become more conscious of the feelings and actions they constructed in order to deal with the experience. Encouraged by the therapist's empathic efforts to understand their experience, they come to understand it and then it is often but a short step to realizing how these constructions are affecting their current functioning.

Many clients present themselves with action-scheme level anger, shame, and sadness (depression) constructions that they have no consciousness of and that severely handicap them in all of their relationships because they assimilate so many events, situations, and objects to these constructions. What is remarkable is that I have encountered this in clients as young as 9 and as old as 70. Some people must be handicapped by these kinds of constructions all of their lives. I have seen it in Ralph, a 9-year-old boy, Jennifer, a woman in her late forties, and Susan, a woman in her late fifties.

Ralph was referred because he was not learning to read and because his angry outbursts were disturbing his teacher and classmates. I saw him in play therapy and he was also being tutored in a small group by a remedial reading teacher. He had a brother who was two years older and doing well in school.

In the playroom, Ralph spent most of his time at the punching bag learning to "defend himself" from the "mean kids" in his classroom. I learned that he was also resisting the remedial reading teacher's efforts to involve him in reading activities. When she could get him to do something, by the next day he would have forgotten it and it was back to square one.

Finally, tiring of punching the bag, Ralph tried other things in the playroom. At this point, I discovered he could not throw darts nor could he catch or throw a ball. What was even more significant was the fact that after one attempt and failure he would not try again. He was adamant about this: No way, he could not do it, and that was that.

It became clear to me that, years before, Ralph had compared his performance with his brother's and concluded that since his first efforts to do something did not equal what his brother could do, that that meant he couldn't do it. He had constructed what was a profound shame construction to which he was assimilating a number of activities. To avoid the shame of failing again, he stopped trying. He was convinced that he could not learn to read or to play ball and, I am sure, a number of other things as well. And when forced to try something he "knew" he could not do, he would get mad. It had become his way of avoiding further shame.

When I recognized this and explained to him that I thought this was what he was doing, he realized that this was what he was, in fact, doing. He agreed to let me show him how to throw a ball and catch one, too. I helped him experience that learning something new is a matter of continuous effort to improve one's skill and that one's first effort is just a beginning that, with practice, will become better and better. Best of all, since he was now trying, I could show him this in action and then we could talk about it.

Ralph made rapid progress and when he then dared to try to learn to read he was soon reading at a third grade level. Shame and anger gave way to joy and pride. This change was accomplished in just a little more than eight months.

When Jennifer was 5 years old, a male neighbor in his twenties began sexually abusing her. After about two years, Jennifer decided that what was happening to her was wrong so she went to great lengths to avoid this man. However, she felt ashamed about what had happened because she thought it was her fault. She was too scared to talk to either parent and an older sister, although supportive, couldn't really help her.

Jennifer came to see me because she had read a newspaper article about me that described my interest in emotional development. She hoped that I could help her "get to the bottom of" why she had these strange feelings that she didn't understand, and why she was having so much trouble in all of her relationships.

After about twenty minutes in my office, Jennifer began weeping quietly and she held her hand up to cover her face as she talked with me. I recognized that she had an action-scheme level shame construction that was devastating for her. It was clear that most of her relationships were spoiled by her need for reassurance that others really were interested in her because she was sure that they wouldn't be if they *really* knew her. She was not conscious of her shame or of what she was doing that made people so uncomfortable with her.

By our fourth session, I was able to tell Jennifer what I thought was happening to her and what she was doing, at which point she had a long cry because she was so relieved to finally understand what she was caught up in. (Other therapists she had seen over the years had been of help, but not with what was "really wrong," as she put it.)

Jennifer's weeping stopped. She no longer hid her face when we talked about all the ways her feeling of shame and her ways of acting upon this feeling were keeping her from having the kinds of relationships she wanted to have.

Susan had a very difficult childhood. Her father gave her little attention and her mother let her know when she had done something wrong by assaulting her verbally and physically. Hearing nothing but criticism, Susan became very critical of just about everything herself. She had an anger construction into which she assimilated everything that wasn't what it "should" be.

Susan had been married three times. Her current marriage had been floundering lately, so I began seeing Susan and her husband, Robert, together. Robert really cared about Susan and wanted to make the marriage work.

Susan was hypersensitive to all slights and all actions that she believed to be inconsiderate. Typically, Robert was puzzled by her rage so he would withdraw, which threatened her even more. "Damn!" she would say, "He won't even fight with me!"

At first, my attempts to help Susan understand what she was doing were taken as criticism of her. "You're just blaming me for everything. What about him?"

We got past that in just a few hours and both of them began to understand why what they had been doing was not working. They had not been responding to each other's needs. Susan began to understand her anger and why she was so threatened by so many things. Robert became more supportive and more attentive.

For Jennifer it was shame and for Susan it was anger; both had action-scheme level feeling-action constructions of which they were not conscious. My questions proved to be very helpful to them. The questions and my efforts to help them understand what they were doing became a significant part of their self-reflective consciousness.

As I am sure you can tell, I believe it is very therapeutic and ethical as well to explain to clients my best understanding of the cause of their discomfort. I always add to this some description of what I believe they must do (or what we must do jointly) for them to achieve their therapeutic goals. I also give them my best estimate of the time that will be required for them to achieve these objectives.

However, I do regard these explanations and estimates as working hypotheses and I do not hesitate to change them as my work with my clients progresses. For example, when I first saw Susan and Robert I estimated that it would probably take two years to achieve their therapeutic goals. After eighteen hours over a five-month period, it was obvious to them and to me that they had realized their objectives.

On the other hand, with a 50-year-old client I shall call Bob, my first estimate was that our work together would take twelve to eighteen months. I saw Bob for three years. Bob was a very intelligent man with a graduate degree from a prestigious university, but both of his parents had been alcoholic and he had virtually no understanding of why he had gotten into serious difficulties twenty years earlier. My hypothesis about the cause of his personality disorder changed several times in the course of my work with him. The EDI questions and my empathic effort to understand him enabled Bob to make remarkable gains in his emotional maturity.

Treatment for Victims of Trauma and Abuse

The treatment of children traumatized by violence was described earlier. These same treatment principles apply to the treatment of other children, and adults as well, who have had or who are in the midst of a traumatic experience. Warmth and support are important, but it is especially important that these victims cognize their experience of the trauma. Getting them to describe, talk about, and clarify how they feel about the experience, and then to review and discuss what they are going to do—what they *must* do to integrate the experience and get on with their lives—is essential.

A period of sadness or grieving may be necessary, but making a "career" out of having been a victim should be discouraged.

At some point, victims must be challenged to decide how they want to relate to their experience and then therapists must help them to become conscious of how their way of adapting to this experience is affecting their current relationships. Victims must be encouraged to construct realistic feelings and effective ways of acting upon these feelings if they are to recover from their traumatic experience.

For the victims of abuse, which can be considered a form of trauma, I am not at all sure that either catharsis or getting together with other victims and reliving the experience again and again is useful. Also, the practice of encouraging clients to remember their abuse and convincing some clients that they were abused does not make sense in the context of this neo-Piagetian theory. The memory, itself, is not important. What is important is for clients to become conscious of the feelings and emotions they constructed as a way of relating to their abuse and abuser. Have they spent their lives assimilating their experience of other people to these constructions? How did they feel about the abuse then? How do they feel about the abuse now? They were probably young and essentially without power then. How would they deal with such behavior now? Helping clients to become conscious of how what they did then is affecting what they do now is the most important thing the therapist can do.

Helping victims to forgive those who have abused them is also important. Forgiving involves more than simply finding excuses for the abuser's actions. It is not to be taken lightly nor should it be encouraged too soon in treatment. Courtois (1988) provides an excellent discussion of forgiveness and she calls attention to Fitzgibbons' longer discussion of this topic in which he makes the following observation: "Emotional forgiveness, that is, when one truly feels like forgiving another, is normally preceded by a significant amount of time and energy spent in intellectual forgiving" (p. 348).

Courtois (1988) also states that in her experience working with incest survivors not all of them were able to forgive their abusers, but then she makes this cogent observation: "If a survivor cannot forgive, she must have enough resolution or disengagement from the past to be able to claim her present and future for herself. She must not remain stuck in futile anger but rather must use it as a spur to her development" (p. 349).

These basic principles also apply in the treatment of those who have experienced physical and emotional abuse. One problem often encountered in treating these victims is their belief that they deserved the abuse because they were, in fact, "bad," "evil," "dumb," or "stupid." The profound sense of shame that many victims of this kind of abuse have is often hidden by anger and contempt; that is, these victims feel anger and contempt for themselves as "unworthy" or "no good" and these feelings may move them to actions that they hope will remove their sense of shame. They are often not conscious of these feelings and they end up puzzled because they were angry and contemptuous, and their shame remains.

Treatment programs for victims of trauma and abuse should be carefully planned and implemented. I have seen victims of abuse with the additional problem of having to forgive themselves for having participated in the abuse. They feel ashamed because they enjoyed it at first, and they became angry and felt exploited only as they got older.

Victims of emotional incest have an especially difficult situation. Having been the favored, chosen child (treated as a peer by a parent) these children do not feel like victims—after all, they had it all. Only later, having left the incestuous relationship, does life become difficult for them. They keep expecting to be treated by others as "special" and when this does not happen, they may become depressed. Love (1990) has called attention to this syndrome and its treatment.

Addictions and Dependencies

In the theoretical context I am developing here, when working with people with various addictions and dependencies it is important to recognize that their addictions or dependencies meet a significant need. In fact, most addictive and dependent behavior is a way of life organized around certain patterns of social behavior. These patterns become very fixed and include a number of action-scheme level feeling-action constructions into which most of the person's experience is assimilated, thus creating what is essentially a closed system. Breaking out of this closed system is very difficult for some people. When the decision to do so is made, however, a program of emotional reeducation and/or therapy is essential.

While there are many good recovery programs, most of them would benefit from a program component that focuses on emotional education/emotional development therapy. Those recovering from addictions or dependencies have some unique needs, but with respect to their emotional development they are living in the same system of shared meaning as the rest of us.

CONCLUDING COMMENTS

When talking with us about their emotions, clients give us two important things that we can work with. One is their feelings: Are they clear about how they feel? And, are their feelings sufficiently differentiated and socially appropriate? Do they simply feel good or bad about selected events and situations, or are they appropriately angry, guilty, or sad? I have been surprised by how some clients make only very simple differentiations in their feelings; they feel good, bad, pleased, or sorry. They have a very concrete and limited vocabulary for feelings because they have a very undifferentiated system of values.

It is often necessary to help clients examine and clarify their feelings. I have found it helpful to suggest that they ask others about how they feel in selected situations and to practice being more observant and sensitive to feelings. I have even recommended that they see selected movies so that we can talk about the feelings and emotions experienced by the characters in these movies. For example, two movies I have found to be very helpful are *An Officer and a Gentleman* for its depiction of anger and rage, and *Men Don't Leave* for its depiction of sadness and depression. Some clients need to become more psychologically-minded and more aware of the role that feelings have in their lives.

The other thing clients give us to work with is the logic and ethics of their actions. The action component of our emotions, especially our negative emotions, is very important for our well-being. The actions through which we "express" our feelings either work for us or they don't. They are productive and constructive or they are unproductive, destructive, and sometimes even ineffective; they just prolong stress and discomfort; and sometimes they make the situation worse. By our questions and our efforts to understand, we help clients to become self-reflectively conscious of how effective their actions are and, in the process, help them to achieve emotional maturity.

Just as our way of doing therapy is related to our personal psychology and emotional maturity, so is the average person's way of living related to his or her personal psychology and emotional maturity. Many people have a sound personal psychology and an adequate level of emotional maturity. Nevertheless, from time to time they need psychological assistance and when they ask for it they are easy to work with.

On the other hand, some people have a very unsound personal psychology or none at all, and their emotional development is severely retarded. They are fixated at the action level of consciousness and they express their needs through somatic symptoms or they act out their needs in socially inappropriate ways. They become ill or injured because they are living a life that is psychologically unsound or unworkable, so they show up periodically at emergency services or they commit petty crimes and end up in jail.

Working with these people in psychotherapy is very difficult. They are often exploitive and demanding, and the psychology they live by does not include asking for psychological assistance. They want immediate material help. Then, too, I have seen people (including some very bright people) resist therapy because the very process was in conflict with their personal psychology. Their resistance was conceptual in nature and not with the particulars of the process (sometimes religious beliefs are involved).

Assisting these people with their emotional development has to include helping them to both acquire a psychology that is conceptually sound, and learn to clarify and articulate their feelings and then to act on them in ways that are both personally satisfying and socially appropriate. One might say that they need a remedial psychology course as a prerequisite for emotional education or emotional reconstruction therapy.

Several years ago, as a visiting professor at the University of Rhode Island, I taught Psychology 101 for non-psychology majors. The textbook for the course, *Choice and Change* (O'Connell &

O'Connell, 1980), focused on how psychology applies to real life. It was written for laymen interested in a psychology course that would help them understand themselves. It proved to be one of my most interesting and satisfying teaching experiences.

All but two of the students were between 35 and 50 years of age. Some of them were in recovery programs, several had recovered from "nervous breakdowns," and all of them had problems with their marriages or with their children. The two young people in the class felt out of place and said so, to the good-natured amusement of their older classmates.

The class met for three hours once a week, and I allowed at least an hour for discussion each class meeting. It was never enough. They were highly motivated students and they "ate the course up." They did well on the tests, and several of them appeared to make very real personal gains—stating that the course had given them a whole new outlook on life. The course evaluations were consistently positive.

I felt then, and I feel even more strongly now, that courses of this kind, which would provide the average person the best that our profession has to offer on how to live well psychologically and emotionally, could make a substantial contribution to our emotional well-being as a society. They could lessen the requests for emergency services and reduce petty crime. They would make more people ready to avail themselves of the psychological services we do have to offer and it could lessen the need for long-term treatment.

If more members of our society had an essentially sound personal psychology and emotional maturity, short-term therapy would be all that most people would ever need.

This possibility—I admit it is just that—raises a question I have to ask. As we add to our knowledge in psychology, should we spend our time and energy getting this new knowledge into the hands of practitioners who treat people after the delay in their emotional development has become symptomatic or should we devote more of our time and energy to making this knowledge available to the general public? Over the long run, which would be more cost effective? Or, would some combination of these two efforts be more productive?

As much as I enjoy my work as a therapist in dialogue with some very interesting people, I believe that as a profession we should make a concerted effort to have deliberate psychological and emotional education courses taught in our elementary, middle schools, high schools, community colleges, and adult education programs. Is this not an idea whose time has come?

6

In Search of Emotional Maturity

And the most important task we now face, I feel, is that of determining what we are going to do with ourselves in the future. (Shotter, 1975, p. 134)

Each chapter in this book is considered to be a work in progress. As noted in Chapter 1, Berk (1989) suggests that good theory is important because it tells us what to observe and how the products of our observation are related, provides order and meaning to our research efforts, and provides us with rational guides to practical action. The theory I have presented here does all of these things to some extent:

1. It tells us what to observe. The theory suggests that to understand feelings and emotions and their development, we must talk to the developing person about their reasons for their feelings and their actions upon these feelings in the process of observing their evolving consciousness and the logic of their respective feelings and emotions.

   The theory also tells us how to identify the needs and values that inform feelings and emotions, and how these same needs and values influence a person's choice of action as a way of expressing the value judgment inherent in his or her feelings.

2. The theory tells us how social experience and the construction of our consciousness is related to the logic and, therefore, the effectiveness of our respective emotions. It tells us how this functional relationship is transformed in the course of our emotional development in the service of our intrapersonal and interpersonal equilibrium.

3. The theory provides us with a research tool, the EDI, which gives us questions to ask subjects at all ages about their reasons for their feelings and emotions, thus revealing their evolving consciousness and the status of their emotional development.

Identifying this sequence of questions and their relationship to the theory of emotional development presented here is the product of years of thought, research, and analysis, but it has focused on a selected number of feelings and emotions with a limited number of subjects.

The EDI does, however, produce a unique outcome; it alters our consciousness at the same time that it reveals the status of our emotional development. Now, with the interview as the primary research tool, we are in a position to study emotional development at all age levels, knowing that we are actually contributing, in a small way, to the emotional development of the subjects we are studying.

Obviously we should study more feelings and emotions across the entire span of human development. I believe we should also be studying the influence of gender, culture, social experience, and education on emotional development.

4. The theory provides us with practical guides for emotional education and for psychotherapy. It seems clear that the EDI is both an assessment tool and a mini-therapy session at the same time, thus lending itself to use for brief or time-limited therapy and long-term therapy as well.

The theory suggests a content focus and procedures to be followed in emotional education programs that could facilitate emotional development at the elementary school, middle school, and high school levels. These programs would emphasize a "positive" and "deliberate" effort to encourage and foster the construction of a self-reflective level of consciousness and the construction of effective ways of coping with the core issues in each of our emotions.

The theory has made a considerable contribution to my effectiveness as a psychotherapist, as the cases mentioned in Chapter 5 illustrate. The theory and its application in treatment work has proven in various workshops to be understandable and teachable. Its full potential remains to be explored.

In constructing this theory, my goal was to create a human science of emotional development that includes the achievement of a self-reflective consciousness, and of a repertoire of socially relevant and effective feelings and emotions that could make us more fully human. We need a psychology of human development that puts development and the treatment of development gone awry on the same continuum.

My search for a theory of emotional development led me to examine many of the basic assumptions in the psychology of human development. This, in turn, led me to the recognition that we cannot understand people as objects of nature when, in reality, they are active agents in the process of becoming human beings in a culture created by other human beings.

Thus, the science of human development must be a science that studies people in the process of becoming human beings that share a culture with other human beings and not as a science that studies people as objects of nature. We do begin as objects of nature, but we soon become more than that—we become human selves in relationships with other human selves. We are compelled to live in relationships with other human selves for the duration of our lives, and we must therefore be concerned with the ethics of our actions. This is primarily what the construction of our consciousness and the logic of our feelings and emotions is all about. The study of emotional development must begin with the assumption that we are agents of ethical actions becoming human beings in a culture of shared meaning.

There are an increasing number of articles and books being written on the psychology of specific emotions; for example, Gaylin (1984) on rage; Averill (1982) and Tavris (1989) on anger; Wurmser (1981), Harper and Hoopes (1990), and Karen (1992) on shame; Madow (1988) and Borysenko (1990) on guilt; Beck, Rush, Shaw, and Emery (1979) and Gut (1989) on depression; and Csikszentmihalyi (1990) and Myers (1992) on happiness.

The fact that these emotions are regarded as different and as serving different functions is consistent with my theory, but none of these authors trace the development of these emotions nor the age at which they can be expected to be mature. I have a strong hunch that the middle school through the high school years are critical for emotional development. At this age (13 through 18) children are achieving the formal operations level of abstract thinking, and they have many opportunities for the kinds of social experience that could contribute to a self-reflective consciousness and the development of a full repertoire of effective and constructive feelings and emotions. However, if social experience during this age period is dominated by fear, anxiety, and rage, their development may be seriously distorted or fixated at an immature level.

What I am suggesting is that the theory of emotional development presented here has most of the elements of a new paradigm centered in the notion that our feelings and emotions are personal-social constructions that are informed by our needs and values and made real in a culture of shared meaning. In the context of this new way of looking at our feelings and emotions—this new paradigm—a number of research questions seem meaningful to me.

In addition to our efforts to build models of the development of our various emotions, and perhaps models for the different genders and models for the different cultures, there are questions relating to how emotional development is best nurtured in the home, day care center, preschool, and the K-12 school experience.

Then there is the question of emotional education. Should we be making a more deliberate, positive effort to facilitate emotional development in all of our educational programs, including college and vocational training programs? There is a good chance that these programs would reduce some of the abuse and violence that seem to be on the increase in our society.

If our feelings and emotions are personal-social constructions, and I believe that they are, then perhaps we should take Shotter's (1975) challenge seriously. What are we going to do with ourselves in the future?

With courage and a determined effort, we could all develop a more comprehensive and flexible repertoire of feelings and emotions—feelings that reflect greater sensitivity and empathy for one another, and emotions that involve more effective ways of managing threats to our well-being and identity, our failures and losses, our doubts about our worthiness, and our belief that we have harmed others. We could also do what we must do to develop a greater sense of personal and social pride, and a more widespread feeling of happiness. These emotions are all informed by the values we acquire and nurture for ourselves and for our children.

But we must recognize that not all change is positive. If our values are changing, and it appears that they are, we could become less sensitive and empathic toward one another. We could create the conditions for the construction of more fear, anxiety, and rage, and for a narrower, more restricted and less flexible repertoire of feelings and emotions that would express our society-wide fascination with exploitation, harassment, abuse, and violence.

If our contemporary literature as manifested in the media is accurately reflecting American cultural values, then our culture is in a dangerous decline and this fact will soon be evident in the feelings and emotions our children construct as they adapt to this decline.

Our future and that of our children is at stake—it could go either way. The choice is ours to make. I invite you to join me in the search for emotional maturity.

References

Albee, G. W. (1993, Spring). The answer is prevention. *Psychology Today*, pp. 86–90.

Anand, K.J.S., & Hickey, P. R. (1992). Halothane-morphine compared with high-dose sufentanil for anesthesia and postoperative analgesia in neonatal cardiac surgery. *The New England Journal of Medicine, 326*, 1–9.

Anthony, E. J. (1976a). How children cope in families with a psychotic parent. In E. N. Rexford, L. W. Sander, & T. Shapiro (Eds.), *Infant psychiatry: A new synthesis* (pp. 239–247). New Haven, CT: Yale University Press.

Anthony, E. J. (1976b). Emotions and intelligence. In V. P. Varma & P. Williams (Eds.), *Piaget, psychology and education* (pp. 43–54). London, England: Hodder and Stoughton.

Arnold, M. (1960). *Emotion and personality: Vol. 1. Psychological aspects.* New York: Columbia University Press.

Averill, J. R. (1982). *Anger and aggression: An essay on emotion.* New York: Springer-Verlag.

Barrett, K. C., & Campos, J. J. (1987). Perspectives on emotional development II: A functionalist approach to emotions. In I. B. Weiner (Ed.), *Handbook of infant development* (2nd ed., pp. 555–578). New York: John Wiley & Sons.

Beck, A. T. (1976). *Cognitive therapy and the emotional disorders.* New York: International Universities Press.

Beck, A. T., Rush, A. J., Shaw, B. F., & Emery, G. (1979). *Cognitive therapy of depression.* New York: Guilford Press.

Belenky, M. F., Clinchy, B. M., Goldberger, N. R., & Tarule, J. M. (1986). *Women's ways of knowing.* New York: Basic Books.

Berk, L. E. (1989). *Child development.* Needham Heights, MA: Allyn and Bacon.

Borysenko, J. (1990). *Guilt is the teacher, love is the lesson.* New York: Warner Books.

Branden, N. (1969). *The psychology of self-esteem.* New York: Bantam Books.

Bringuier, J. C. (1980). *Conversations with Jean Piaget.* Chicago: The University of Chicago Press.

Bronowski, J. (1973). *The ascent of man.* Boston: Little, Brown.

Bruner, J. (1983). *In search of mind.* New York: Harper & Row.

Bruner, J. (1990). *Acts of meaning.* Cambridge, MA: Harvard University Press.

Courtois, C. A. (1988). *Healing the incest wound: Adult survivors in therapy.* New York: W. W. Norton.

Csikszentmihalyi, M. (1990). *Flow: The psychology of optimal experience.* New York: Harper & Row.

Dunn, J., & Brown, J. (1991). Relationships, talk about feelings, and the development of affect regulation in early childhood. In J. Garber & K. A. Dodge (Eds.), *The development of emotion regulation and dysregulation* (pp. 89–108). Cambridge, England: Cambridge University Press.

Dupont, H. (1957). Emotional maladjustment and special education. *Exceptional Children, 24,* 10–15.

Dupont, H. (1968). Social learning theory and the treatment of transvestite behavior in an eight year old boy. *Psychotherapy: Theory, Research and Practice, 5,* 44–45.

Dupont, H. (Ed.). (1969). *Educating emotionally disturbed children: Readings.* New York: Holt, Rinehart and Winston.

Dupont, H. (Ed.). (1975). *Educating emotionally disturbed children: Readings* (2nd ed.). New York: Holt, Rinehart and Winston.

Dupont, H. (1978). Meeting the emotional-social needs of children in the mainstream environment. *Human Counseling and Development, 10,* 1–11.

Dupont, H. (1979a). Affective development: A Piagetian model. In M. K. Poulsen & G. I. Lubin (Eds.), *Proceedings 8th annual conference: Piagetian theory and its implications for the helping professions* (pp. 64–71). Los Angeles: USC Bookstore.

Dupont, H. (1979b). Affective development: Stage and sequence (a Piagetian interpretation). In R. L. Mosher (Ed.), *Adolescents' development and education* (pp. 163–183). Berkeley: McCutchan.

Dupont, H. (1989). The emotional development of exceptional students. *Focus on Exceptional Children, 21*(9), 1–10.

Dupont, H., & Dupont, C. (1979). *Transition.* Circle Pines, MN: American Guidance Service.

Dupont, H., Gardner, O. S., & Brody, D. (1974). *Toward affective development.* Circle Pines, MN: American Guidance Service.

Dupont, H. J., Landsman, T., & Valentine, M. (1953). The treatment of delayed speech by client-centered therapy. *Journal of Consulting Psychology, 27,* 122–125.

Eckholm, E. (1992, November 4). Study tries to determine effects on kids of having working mom. *Star Tribune,* p. 7E.

Ellis, A. (1962). *Reason and emotion in psychotherapy.* New York: Lyle Stuart.

Ellis, A. (1985). Cognition and affect in emotional disturbance. *American Psychologist, 40,* 471–472.

Elson, M. (Ed.). (1987). *The Kohut seminars on self psychology and psychotherapy with adolescents and young adults.* New York: W. W. Norton.

Gallagher, J. M., & Reid, D. K. (1981). *The learning theory of Piaget and Inhelder.* Monterey, CA: Brooks/Cole.

Garber, J., & Dodge, K. A. (Eds.). (1991). *The development of emotion regulation and dysregulation.* New York: Cambridge University Press.

Gaylin, W. (1979). *Feelings: Our vital signs.* New York: Harper & Row.

Gaylin, W. (1984). *The rage within.* New York: Simon and Schuster.

Gaylin, W. (1990). *On being and becoming human.* New York: Penguin Books.

Gilligan, C. (1982). *In a different voice.* Cambridge, MA: Harvard University Press.

Gilligan, C., Lyons, N. P., & Hanmer, T. J. (Eds.). (1990). *Making connections.* Cambridge, MA: Harvard University Press.

Gregory, R. L. (Ed.). (1987). *The Oxford companion to the mind.* New York: Oxford University Press.

Gruber, H. E., & Vonèche, J. J. (1977). *The essential Piaget.* New York: Basic Books.

Gut, E. (1989). *Productive and unproductive depression.* New York: Basic Books.

Guthrie, E. R. (1938). *The psychology of human conflict.* New York: Harper & Brothers.

Harper, J. M., & Hoopes, M. H. (1990). *Uncovering shame.* New York: W. W. Norton.

Harré, R. (Ed.). (1986). *The social construction of emotions.* Oxford, England: Basil Blackwell.

Harris, P. L., & Saarni, C. (1989). Children's understanding of emotion: An introduction. In C. Saarni & P. L. Harris (Eds.), *Children's understanding of emotion* (pp. 3–24). New York: Cambridge University Press.

Hobson, R. F. (1985). *Forms of feeling: The heart of psychotherapy.* London, England: Tavistock Publications.

Izard, C. E. (1977). *Human emotions.* New York: Plenum Press.

Izard, C. E., & Malatesta, C. Z. (1987). Perspectives on emotional development I: Differential emotions theory of early emotional development. In J. D. Osofsky (Ed.), *Handbook of infant development* (2nd ed., pp. 494–554). New York: Cambridge University Press.

Janet, P. (1925). *Psychological healing.* New York: Macmillan.

Jordan, J. V. (1993, April). *Increasing empathy: Decreasing shame.* Paper presented at the annual meeting of the Georgia Psychological Association, Atlanta, GA.

Jordan, J. V., Kaplan, A. G., Miller, J. B., Stiver, I. P., & Surrey, J. L. (1991). *Women's growth in connection.* New York: The Guilford Press.

Kagan, J. (1984). *The nature of the child.* New York: Basic Books.

Karen, R. (1992, February). Shame. *The Atlantic Monthly,* pp. 40–70.

Kaufman, G. (1992). *Shame: The power of caring.* Rochester, VT: Schenkman Books.

Lazarus, R. S. (1991a). Progress on a cognitive-motivational-relational theory of emotion. *American Psychologist, 46,* 819–834.

Lazarus, R. S. (1991b). *Emotion and adaptation.* New York: Oxford University Press.

Lewis, M., & Michalson, L. (1983). *Children's emotions and moods: Developmental theory and measurement.* New York: Plenum Press.

Love, P. (1990). *The emotional incest syndrome.* New York: Bantam Books.

Lutz, C. (1987). Goals, events, and understanding in Ifaluk emotion theory. In D. Holland & N. Quinn (Eds.), *Cultural models in language and thought* (pp. 290–312). Cambridge, England: Cambridge University Press.

Madow, L. (1988). *Guilt: How to recognize and cope with it.* Northvale, NJ: Jason Aronson.

Maslow, A. H. (1971). *The farther reaches of human nature.* New York: The Viking Press.

Middelton-Moz, J. (1990). *Shame and guilt: The masters of disguise.* Deerfield Beach, FL: Health Communications.

Myers, D. G. (1992). *The pursuit of happiness.* New York: William Morrow.

O'Connell, A., & O'Connell, V. (1980). *Choice and change: The psychology of adjustment, growth, and creativity.* Englewood Cliffs, NJ: Prentice-Hall.

Paley, V. G. (1984). *Boys and girls: Superheroes in the doll corner.* Chicago: University of Chicago Press.

Piaget, J. (1951). *Play, dreams and imitation in childhood.* New York: W. W. Norton.

Piaget, J. (1952). Jean Piaget. In E. Boring (Ed.), *History of psychology in autobiography* (pp. 237–256). New York: Russell & Russell.

Piaget, J. (1962). The relation of affectivity to intelligence in the mental development of the child. *Bulletin of the Menninger Clinic, 26,* 129–137.

Piaget, J. (1967). *Six psychological studies.* New York: Random House.

Piaget, J. (1971). *Biology and knowledge.* Chicago: University of Chicago Press.

Piaget, J. (1972). *Psychology of intelligence.* Totowa, NJ: Littlefield, Adams.

Piaget, J. (1976a). Affective unconscious and cognitive unconscious. In J. Piaget (Ed.), *The child and reality* (pp. 31–48). New York: Penguin Books.

Piaget, J. (1976b). *The grasp of consciousness: Action and concept in the young child.* Cambridge, MA: Harvard University Press.

Piaget, J. (1977). *The development of thought: Equilibration of cognitive structures.* New York: Viking Press.

Piaget, J. (1981). *Intelligence and affectivity: Their relationship during child development.* Palo Alto, CA: Annual Reviews.

Piaget, J., & Inhelder, B. (1969). *The psychology of the child.* New York: Basic Books.

Potter-Efron, R., & Potter-Efron, P. (1989). *Letting go of shame.* New York: Harper & Row.

Rokeach, M. (1973). *The nature of human values.* New York: The Free Press.

Rosaldo, M. Z. (1980). *Knowledge and passion.* Cambridge, England: Cambridge University Press.

Ruch, F. L., & Zimbardo, P. G. (1971). *Psychology and life* (8th ed.). Glenview, IL: Scott, Foresman.

Saarni, C., & Harris, P. L. (Eds.). (1989). *Children's understanding of emotion.* New York: Cambridge University Press.

Shotter, J. (1975). *Images of man in psychological research.* London, England: Methuen.

Shotter, J. (1984). *Social accountability and selfhood.* New York: Basil Blackwell.

Solomon, R. C. (1983). *The passions: The myth and nature of human emotion.* Notre Dame, IN: University of Notre Dame Press.

Sroufe, L. A. (1979). Socioemotional development. In J. D. Osofsky (Ed.), *The handbook of infant development* (pp. 462–515). New York: John Wiley & Sons.

Tavris, C. (1989). *Anger: The misunderstood emotion.* New York: Simon & Schuster.

Tomkins, S. S. (1962). *Affect, imagery, consciousness: Vol. 1. The positive affects.* New York: Springer.

Tomkins, S. S. (1963). *Affect, imagery, consciousness: Vol. 2. The negative affects.* New York: Springer.

Tomkins, S. S. (1987). Shame. In D. L. Nathanson (Ed.), *The many faces of shame* (pp. 133–163). New York: Guilford Press.

Vannicelli, M. (1989). *Group psychotherapy with adult children of alcoholics.* New York: Guilford Press.

Weiner, B., Runquist, W., Runquist, P. A., Raven, B. H., Meyer, W. J., Leiman, A., Kutscher, C. L., Kleinmuntz, B., & Haber, R. N. (1977). *Discovering psychology.* Chicago: Science Research Associates.

White, B. L., & Watts, J. C. (1973). *Experience and environment: Vol. 1. Major influences on the development of the young child.* Englewood Cliffs, NJ: Prentice-Hall.

Wurmser, L. (1981). *The mask of shame.* Baltimore: Johns Hopkins University.

Index

About the Author

HENRY DUPONT, a practicing psychotherapist at Atlanta Area Psychological Associates, has taught at the University of Wisconsin-Eau Claire and at the University of Hawaii. He has had extensive experience as an author, educator, and psychotherapist for both children and adults, with a lifelong interest in emotional development. He has is the author of *Assessing Emotional Development* (1982); the senior author of *Transition: A Curriculum Program to Help Students Through the Difficult Passage from Childhood to Middle Adolescence* (1979) and *Toward Affective Development* (1974); and the editor of *Educating Emotionally Disturbed Children* (1974, 1969).